THE MENTORS
AMONG US

THE MENTORS AMONG US

Cases in the Human Services

Melissa Rothwell and *Kelly Mazerolle*

Toronto | Vancouver

The Mentors Among Us: Cases in the Human Services
Melissa Rothwell and Kelly Mazerolle

First published in 2018 by
Canadian Scholars, an imprint of CSP Books Inc.
425 Adelaide Street West, Suite 200
Toronto, Ontario
M5V 3C1

www.canadianscholars.ca

Library and Archives Canada Cataloguing in Publication

Rothwell, Melissa, 1982-, author
    The mentors among us : cases in the human services / Melissa Rothwell and Kelly Mazerolle.

Includes bibliographical references.
Issued in print and electronic formats.
ISBN 978-1-77338-027-8 (softcover).—ISBN 978-1-77338-028-5 (PDF).—ISBN 978-1-77338-029-2 (EPUB)

    1. Human services—Case studies. I. Mazerolle, Kelly, 1971-, author II. Title.

HV40.R72 2018   361   C2018-902703-7
                                                        C2018-902704-5

Cover and text design by Elisabeth Springate
Typesetting by Hope Thompson
Cover image by Christine Genest, 2017

Printed and bound in Canada by Webcom

MIX
Paper from
responsible sources
FSC® C004071

ABOUT THE COVER ARTIST: CHRISTINE GENEST

Born in Victoriaville in 1970, Christine became interested in the arts
when she was nine years old. She began exploring ceramics, then painting,
drawing, sculpture, and many other forms. A self-taught painter, she has
a sensitivity for art and expresses her artistic side in naïve art. Her work
is inspired by the meeting of the real and imaginary worlds.

CONTENTS

Jean-Stéphane's Story   107

Family support coordinator

Key themes: *parental rights, child welfare, protection services*

Renée's Story   119

Child care centre supervisor

Key themes: *custody, positive-behaviour supports, inclusive care plans, parenting styles*

Isabelle's Story   133

Intake worker at a shelter

Key themes: *abuse, human rights, grief, documentation*

Conclusion: Jamal's Story   147

Director at a seniors' assisted living facility

Key themes: *intergenerational, ageism, social isolation, working with seniors*

Appendices   155

ACKNOWLEDGEMENTS

We would both like to thank our mentor, matthew heinz, from Royal Roads University, and our colleagues at Lakeland College for their support during this adventure. Special thanks to Joanne McDonald for her insight and encouragement. We would also like to thank Bruce Northey at the College of New Caledonia and another anonymous reviewer who provided valuable feedback and advice on an earlier version of the manuscript.

I would like to thank my mother, Marise, for encouraging me to always reach for the stars. To my husband, Sam, and my son, Hunter, thank you for your endless support and encouragement. M.R.

With love and gratitude to my parents, Ken and Henrietta, for encouraging my love of reading; to my husband, Steve, for making the world a better place; and my children, Mackinlay and Loganne, for teaching me to have faith and to think outside of the box. K.M.

INTRODUCTION

In the field of human services, front line workers face challenging situations and make decisions that have an impact not only on their lives but also on the lives of their clients. In order to make those decisions effectively, human services professionals rely on their education and experience. Human services is defined as an interdisciplinary knowledge base that focuses on prevention, remediation of problems, and improving the lives of vulnerable people (National Organization for Human Services, n.d., para. 1). The field of human services is quite broad and involves a number of relationships with colleagues, clients, and other organizations. "Human services is not a single service delivery system but a complex web of helping agencies and organizations whose primary goal is to assist people in need" (Woodside & McClam, 2015, p. 17). The umbrella of services, or—as we have illustrated on the cover of our book—the roof under which we provide services, includes a wide range of supports, such as parental and family support and intervention, services for immigrants and refugees, early intervention programs, shelters, mental health agencies, judicial systems, foster families, trauma programs, safe zones, education centres, and mentoring programs. The people who work in the field use their knowledge and skills to make a positive change in the world.

Having taught at the college level in the department of human services, the authors, Melissa and Kelly, noticed that the students enjoy hearing about real life experiences not only from the teachers when they were front line workers but from people who are currently working in the field. "A mentor, therefore, has always been considered one who draws upon a deep knowledge base to teach and guide" (Swap, Leonard, Shields, & Abrams, 2001, p. 98). The individuals who were asked to tell their stories for this publication are all human services

Therapeutic Milieu
Source: C. Genest

professionals who share their experiences, both positive and negative, in order to help the readers to connect the theory they are learning with what is actually happening in the field. Often, these professionals become trusted mentors, and the sharing of expertise and advice is something that is not taken for granted in a career path that can be complex. Learning from the experiences of others can help current professionals to develop a skillset that provides them with a level of competency and contributes to their success and longevity in the field. "When novices are immersed in an organization or culture they value, and are being mentored by an expert they admire, a great deal of learning can occur through observing the expert's behaviour" (Swap et al., 2001, p. 102).

As a result, each chapter of this book is designed to feature a mentor talking about an event they have experienced over the course of their career in the human services field. The reader will be asked to become involved in the story by choosing which path they would follow if they were the mentor. In some cases, there are numerous paths that could be taken, but the authors have designed the book to look at two possible options. Every story is based on a real life situation, and one of the pathways was actually followed. This model provides mentorship in an innovative form, rather than a face-to-face, traditional relationship. The reader will follow each mentor's pathway to learn from, question, and reflect upon the mentor's experience.

The authors wish to acknowledge the willingness of the mentors to participate in this project and have taken steps to maintain confidentiality by changing the names and places referred to in each story. This choose-your-own-adventure format gives the reader the ability to experience an event with the guidance of their instructor and the mentor featured within the pages. "Role modelling provides the opportunity for the mentee to observe others and learn from their actions, particularly in relationship to the application of personal values in work settings and strategic tactics used to address problems" (Goodyear, 2006, p. 51). Key concepts provided within each story allow the reader to extract the information needed for their overall knowledge and to develop a clearer understanding of human services. Please note that not all key concepts will be contained within the option the reader has selected. For the "In the Pursuit of Knowledge" sections, the reader will be asked to use critical thinking skills to reflect upon the information provided within each chapter and to think outside of the box by participating in the activities and discussions. As a complement, there is also a companion website with resources, external links, and a virtual version of the mentors' stories that appeals to different instructional and learning styles. At the end of the book, the appendices include blank templates of reports.

A case study research is an in-depth study of a particular situation. The authors seek to provide the reader with the opportunity to think critically and develop their professional identity by analyzing components of adherence to best practices. It is the authors' goal to explore the philosophical paradigms at the foundational level of the human services profession. So take off your rose-coloured glasses, put your thinking cap on, and listen to the mentors among us.

REFERENCES

Goodyear, M. (2006). Mentoring: A learning collaboration. *Educause Quarterly 4*, 51–53. www.educause.edu/ir/library/pdf/eqm0647.pdf

National Organization for Human Services. (n.d.). *What is human services?* Retrieved from www.nationalhumanservices.org/

Swap, W., Leonard, D., Shields, M., & Abrams, L. (2001). Using mentoring and storytelling to transfer knowledge in the workplace. *Journal of Management and Information Systems, 18*(1), 95–114.

Woodside, M., & McClam, T. (2015). *An introduction to the human services* (8th ed.). New York: Cengage.

MATT'S STORY

Hi! My name is Matt. I am a 30-year-old personal support worker for a non-profit community living program. It is a great program that supports teens and adults who have developmental disabilities. I provide residential care to my clients based on what is written in their **individual service plan (ISP)**. An ISP is a document that outlines the supports and services available to the client in order to help them to reach their goals. As a personal support worker, I provide my clients with personal care, escorts to their place of employment, and escorts to community activities. I also assist them with housekeeping duties and focus on providing them with opportunities to achieve the goals set out in their ISPs. In my role, I worked with a client, Geoff, a 21-year-old, severely autistic, non-verbal male transitioning from living at home to independent living. Geoff had just graduated from high school.

Geoff

Source: C. Genest

I had been working with Geoff for about ten months. During this time, we had become very close. When Geoff got up that morning, he was kind of grumpy, like any other 21-year-old. He went to work and he was fine, but during the transition coming home at lunch time . . . well, Geoff became extremely aggressive, pounding on the kitchen walls, hitting the counter, hitting the windows, breaking the glass and getting it all over himself, and he actually hit me. The other worker got scared and went out of the room, leaving me alone with Geoff.

❧

What would you do if you were in Matt's situation? You have two options:

Option 1: Leave. It is all about your personal safety. If you choose this option, turn to page 7.
Option 2: Stay and try to de-escalate the situation. If you choose this option, turn to page 13.

OPTION 1

Since Matt and Geoff's personal safety is at risk, you will need immediate assistance to de-escalate the situation. Leave the house and call 911 from your car. Usually when you call 911, they dispatch an ambulance and a police car. It is important in this case to inform the 911 operator that Geoff may have more violent outbursts due to his exceptionality and to provide the operator with a description of what Geoff is wearing so the first responders will be able to recognize him. You should also give the operator a list of Geoff's medications and any allergies.

While on the phone, you need to stay as calm as possible and follow the operator's instructions. This will help to ensure the safety of the police officers, the paramedics, and your client. When speaking with the 911 operator, you can ask the responders not to use their sirens or turn on their lights once they approach the house if you think that will **trigger** Geoff. Sometimes images, smells, or loud noises can cause a negative reaction such as panic or a seizure in an individual. The client may not be able to control what triggers them and there may not even be any warning signs. A trigger is based on a sensory stimulation that initiates a behavioural response. The response is immediate and usually manifests itself in the form of an observable behaviour. A trigger is very emotionally charged and can lead to both unconscious and conscious responses (Corsini, 1999, p. 1022).

Once the emergency responders arrive, tell them what happened and be there to support them as well as Geoff. Show them your injury so they can determine if you need treatment (City of Toronto, 2015). If you are working for an agency, contact your supervisor to report the incident. You will need to document the incident for their files. The agency should give you an **incident report** form to fill out. Be sure to be objective and respect confidentiality. In order to remain professional and distance yourself from the incident, it would be a good idea to write out a rough draft of the incident, get all of your emotions and frustrations out on paper, and rewrite the description later in the incident report form. Date the form and keep a copy for yourself. Be sure to shred your rough copy or keep it in a password-protected file on your work computer. In some cases, organizations have policies and procedures concerning the storage of confidential files.

After the incident, you should revisit Geoff's individual service plan. His ISP is accessible to his legal guardians and workers. It is intended to support caregivers by providing them with learning strategies to help promote the client's independence and access to specialized services when needed (Family Support for Children with Disabilities, 2013, p. 2). Typically in human services, clients will have a specialized service team. The team should include the client's guardian, health professional, certified teacher, child and youth care worker, social worker, health care aide, and psychiatric aide. It is important to note that the team members can change based on community resources, location, and availability of providers. However, regardless of where a client may reside, human services professionals and health care providers will be a part of the team (FSCD, 2013, p. 3).

An ISP must be straightforward and clear while taking into consideration the guardian's priorities and needs. Do they need respite? Assistance in the home? Specialized equipment? The ISP also includes the client's goals, both short term and long term, and strategies to achieve them. The goals need to be meaningful, measurable, and realistic, taking into account the functional skill level of the client. The roles and responsibilities of all team members should also be outlined in the ISP, as well as a plan to ensure that the services and programs are being monitored and that a reassessment is being conducted on a regular basis (FSCD, 2013, pp. 4–7).

Because we are human services professionals, the decisions we make have an impact on our employer, the children and youth with whom we work, and their families. In some instances, the results of our decisions can be positive and life-changing, or they can cause harm or further trauma. Because Matt made the decision to call 911, Geoff could be charged with aggravated assault. Is this a consequence that Matt would uphold? Would he testify against Geoff? Should Matt report his colleague's actions to his superiors? It is important to use our critical thinking skills and know when to take a step back from a situation when our personal values and professional ethical standards are being compromised.

Ethical decision making has a foundation in philosophy that seeks to address a person's morals and beliefs. Often when considering ethical decision making, moral philosophy is mentioned. **Moral philosophy** refers to the principles that each individual establishes as a benchmark for what is right (moral) and what is wrong (immoral). Moral philosophers sometimes provide hypotheses about how people make decisions (Sheridan, 2016). Hare (1981) believes that people usually make moral judgments based on intuition, but that with time, training, and need, they can make decisions based on analytical thinking (p. 3).

Since this individualistic or group norm is based on belief systems, it is not written in stone. Things change, people change, and there is no common, universal morality. Every branch of human services has its own code of conduct and professional ethical standards that were created based on societal expectations, religious organizations, and the beliefs of the profession, but ultimately it is the individual's personal values that will influence what they decide to do. **Values** are "the principle or moral standards of a person or social group; the generally accepted or personally held judgment of what is valuable or important in life" (Barber, 2005). Our values help determine our professional identity and are often found in our professional code of conduct.

First and foremost, as professionals, we need to identify our own values in order to find work with an agency in a capacity that corresponds to such values. By identifying our core values and examining how they will influence our work as a professional, we will be able to help our clients to the best of our ability while remaining true to ourselves. Always remember that you may not believe what your clients believe, but as long as their actions are not causing them or anyone else harm, you cannot change their values. For example, think of a white supremacist group or a polygamous group. You most likely will not share their values or beliefs, but you are still responsible to work with them, or to find someone in your organization or community who can provide supports for them. The human services profession has its own set of values, which include developing effective strategies for our clients and ourselves in coping with stress; being compassionate but having self-control, honesty, and integrity; and being self-aware (Kenyon, 1999, pp. 4–5).

Jean Piaget (1969) observed children at play and is known for his theory of cognitive development, in which he outlined four stages from birth (sensorimotor stage) to adolescence (formal operational stage). He also published his theory of moral development (1932). Piaget determined that children from age five to nine base their decisions on the resulting consequences. If they are rewarded, it was a right decision. If they are punished, it was a wrong decision. This is known as the moral realism stage. Piaget believed that children do not have their own set of moral beliefs before the age of five, and that during the moral realism stage they base their moral beliefs upon the actions of those who reward or punish them.

The next stage is the moral relativism stage. By age ten, most children have developed their own moral beliefs. They are concerned with what others such as their family and friends think, but take into consideration whether an action is against the law or goes against what society thinks is right. Their determination of what is right or wrong becomes more abstract (Piaget, 1932).

While Piaget believed there are two stages of moral reasoning, Lawrence Kohlberg (1976) wanted to determine whether there were stages in human development pertaining to moral judgment. He presented scenarios and stories to people, including children of various ages from a variety of cultural backgrounds, and came to the conclusion that there are six developmental stages of moral judgment, which he categorized by levels (Baxter & Rarick, 1987, pp. 243–244).

Table 1: Six developmental stages of moral judgment

Level	Description	Stage
I: Preconventional morality	Preconventional reasoning Judgments are based on the behaviour of individuals with authority outside of the self, usually the parents or the guardian.	I: Punishment Follows rules in order to avoid being punished and understands that adults have superior power. II: Individualism Avoids things that are punishable and does things that are rewarded. Follows rules when it is in their best interest and for rewards.
II: Conventional morality	Conventional reasoning Judgments are based on the norms of the societal group to which the individual belongs.	III: Relationships, Interpersonal Expectations, and Conformity Believes that good behaviour makes other people happy. IV: Law and Order, Conscience, and Social System Focuses on doing what they believe to be their duty, respects authority, and follows rules.
III: Postconventional morality	Postconventional reasoning There is a shift in authority in this stage; judgments are based on a person's rights and the needs of society.	V: Social Contract Orientation Law and order are important, but the person at this level acknowledges that sometimes rules can be ignored or changed. VI: Universal Ethical Principles The person weighs moral principles against each other to determine which should be used to solve the issue.

Source: Baxter & Rarick, 1987, pp. 243–244

One of the most difficult things for many people is to weigh the odds and make an ethical decision. In order to make an ethical decision, we need to be aware of our code of conduct, our personal values, and the values of the people we are working with and to have a firm understanding of the implications of our decisions. To help guide your thought process, we have created the following list of things you should take into consideration when making ethical decisions:

1. Who is involved in the decision? This means not only the people making the decision but all the people who would be affected by the process and the decision (the clients, their families, the workers, the organizations, etc.).
2. What is the context? Why do you have to make a decision?
3. What are the legal implications?
4. What are the facts? Always seek additional information if you do not have all the facts.
5. How much time do you have to make a decision? Always allow the time to take everything into consideration.
6. What do the ethical guidelines for the practice of your profession and your organization state?
7. What are the short-term and long-term implications? Is this going to set a precedent? Is the decision only a Band-Aid solution to the problem? Are people going to be harmed as a direct result of your decision?
8. Is there a **conflict of interest**? A conflict of interest is a situation in which a person's "private interests might benefit from his or her public actions or influence" (Barber, 2005).

Do not hesitate to bring a co-worker or your supervisor in on your decision-making process. Talking things through with another person will help you to see the big picture. Sometimes you do not have the authority to make the decision. If this is the case, present the facts to the person who does.

Communication is very important among team members outside of your organization as well as those within, especially when you are placed in a stressful situation. In this case, Matt's co-worker left him alone. This may have been a violation of the code of conduct or organizational policies because Matt could have been severely injured. Both Matt and his co-worker knew about Geoff's violent tendencies and should have developed a **safety plan** when they first started working together. A safety plan is an outline of how you intend to keep your client and yourself safe. It includes some strategies indicating what you would do if a situation like this one, for example, occurs. Some organizations ask that their employees be trained in nonviolent crisis intervention. Human services professionals who take this training learn how to reduce the risk of injury and promote safety for both themselves and the client (Crisis Prevention Institute, 2017).

Many agencies have a policy stating that you cannot work alone. This is for your personal safety. If you were working alone and slipped and hit your head, who would look after the clients? Who would call for help? However, budgets sometimes do not allow for more than one staff member—at opening or closing times, for example. There should be a plan in place, such as a person you can call once you arrive and after you leave, or a way to check in with another employee, in order to make sure that both you and the client are safe.

It is a stressful time in Geoff's life because he has just moved into the house. It is a new environment for him and a new routine now that he has graduated from high school. He was comfortable and familiar with the routine of going to school and living at home. Stress can be positive, such as a new home and new opportunities after graduation, yet this is an unsettling time because everything has changed. Geoff is nonverbal, so you need to spend time encouraging him to express himself, his worries and frustrations, rather than bottling them up inside. Geoff might wring his hands or start rocking back and forth or put his hands over his ears. You need to pick up on the clues that your client is becoming agitated and have strategies to de-escalate the situation. By taking a nonviolent crisis intervention course, you will learn strategies to use with your client during a crisis so they do not harm themselves or the people around them. To prevent situations like this from occurring, your client needs to develop ways to manage stress and so do you. You could go to the gym and work out or go jogging. You could watch a movie, listen to music, or read a book. You could paint or play games on the computer.

Transitions—times when an individual moves from one activity or environment that feels comfortable to another—can be very stressful. It is essential that you prepare Geoff for a transition by giving him a warning, such as, "Five minutes until we have to leave for lunch." A visual schedule showing Geoff arriving at work, taking a coffee break, and leaving for lunch could also be helpful. There are some great computer applications that enable you to create a visual schedule by, for instance, uploading a picture of Geoff putting on his coat or eating lunch. It helps make the concept of time more concrete and establishes a routine, thus creating a sense of security so that Geoff will know what to expect. However, there will always be events that you cannot plan for, such as the fire alarm. Talk to Geoff about what to do and then practice a fire drill to help him become familiar with the process of the drill and the sound of the alarm. Repetition is key!

Once the 911 emergency responders have taken Geoff to the hospital for observation, what's next? **Self-care!** Stress is a condition or feeling that is experienced when a person has exceeded their ability to manage a situation. The person then feels as though they can no longer cope with the pressures that have been placed on them. It is important to avoid accumulating stress, which can lead to burnout, by practising some self-care. The human services field is exciting, emotional, and at times overwhelming. In order to take care of others, you need to take care of yourself.

OPTION 2: MATT'S CHOICE

> Now, my client has verbal cues to de-escalate. If I tell Geoff to sit, for example, he must sit—not on the couch, not on a chair, but on the floor, where he usually continues by ripping his shirt to shreds. But this is typically okay because he does not become aggressive with his care providers. Geoff also learned to look me in the eye to de-escalate, but sometimes this makes things worse because he gets fixated on me or the other support worker. That day at Geoff's house, I had to actually use a form of nonviolent intervention to de-escalate him. This incident led me to quit the job, even though the best part of it was working with Geoff.

What worked for Matt in this option is that he recognized Geoff's trigger. Sometimes images, smells, or loud noises can cause or trigger a negative reaction such as panic or a seizure in an individual. The client may not be able to control what triggers them and there may not even be any warning signs. A trigger is based on a sensory stimulation that initiates a behavioural response. The response is immediate and usually manifests itself in the form of an observable behaviour. A trigger is very emotionally charged and can lead to both unconscious and conscious responses (Corsini, 1999, p. 1022).

Geoff's individual service plan, or ISP, is straightforward and clear. It has a behavioural risk assessment and prevention component that helped keep Matt safe. Geoff's ISP is accessible to his guardian and workers. The family's priorities need to be included. The ISP is intended to support caregivers and includes learning strategies to help promote the client's independence and access to specialized services when needed (Family Support for Children with Disabilities, 2013, p. 2). Typically in human services, clients will have a specialized service team. The team should include the client's guardian, health professional, certified teacher, child and youth care worker, social worker, health care aide, and psychiatric aide. It is important to note that the team members can change based on community resources, location, and availability of providers. However, regardless of where a client may reside, human services professionals and health care providers will be a part of the team. The roles and responsibilities of all team members should also be outlined in the ISP, as well as a plan to ensure that the services and programs are being monitored and that a reassessment is being conducted on a regular basis (Family Support for Children with Disabilities, 2013, pp. 3–7).

By using his critical thinking skills, Matt was able to stay calm and think during a crisis. Critical thinking is a process. It can take some time for an individual to be able to reach their full critical thinking potential. According to Brookfield (1987), critical thinkers are actively engaged, innovative, and creative, and they see the possibilities in life. They view the future as open and are self-confident about their potential. Elder and Paul (2010) discuss the stages of **critical thinking development** in their article *Critical Thinking Development: A Stage Theory*. They believe there are six predictable stages people experience on their way to becoming critical thinkers. The ability to graduate from one stage to

Table 2: Six stages of critical thinking development

Stages	Features
One: *The unreflective thinker*	Unaware of the role that thinking is playing in their lives and the problems it is causing. Lacking the knowledge.
Two: *The challenged thinker*	Become aware of the determining role that thinking has in their lives.
Three: *The beginning thinker*	Actively taking command of their thinking. Begin to change some of their thinking. Lack a systematic plan for finding a method to improve their thinking.
Four: *The practising thinker*	Have a sense of the habits they need to develop to control their thinking. Recognize that there is a problem in their thinking and that they need to systematically and globally attack the problem.
Five: *The advanced thinker*	Have established good habits of thought that are working for them. Actively analyze their thinking in all the significant areas of their lives.
Six: *The accomplished thinker*	Have taken charge of their thinking, are continuously assessing and reassessing strategies for improving their thinking.

Source: Elder & Paul, 2010

the next is dependent upon a specific level of commitment and is not an automatic process. Regression is also a possibility (Elder & Paul, 2010).

Often in this field you will be asked to write your reflections on what happened during an activity or an outing that you planned in the form of a journal or an evaluation. Reflect upon the strengths (what went right), the weaknesses (what went wrong), and what you would change if you were to do it again. Taking the time to reflect on what happened will help to develop your critical thinking skills as well as hone your abilities as a professional.

You chose Option 2, so you need to be aware of the risks associated with the profession. Some of the clients you will work with may have contracted an infectious disease. To protect yourself, consider updating your immunizations, but know that not every infectious disease has a vaccine. If you work with a client who has an infectious disease, ensure that you always use disinfectant, cover their cuts with a plastic bandage, and always wear gloves. In Matt's case, he would make sure that his open wounds from the glass do not come into contact with Geoff's fresh blood. It is extremely important for all organizations to disclose to their workers whether their client has an infectious disease and to provide their workers with the appropriate protective equipment, such as gloves and masks. Remember that you cannot catch HIV, for example, like a common cold. In order to be infected, the blood needs to be fresh; there must be a large quantity of blood and a direct route into the bloodstream of the uninfected person (Canadian Child Care Federation, 2004).

Matt successfully de-escalated the situation with Geoff. What's next? Self-care! Self-care is taking time to put yourself first. We all have something that calms us down. It can be reading a book, going for a walk, or hanging out with some friends. Stress is a condition or feeling that is experienced when a person has exceeded their ability to manage a situation and they feel as though they can no longer cope with the pressures that have been placed on them. It is the body's response to a perceived or real threat. Some stress can be good; it can help motivate us to focus on a task or take action; it can be manageable and a positive thing. But stress is unhelpful when it makes you feel overwhelmed or as though you cannot fix the problems you face. Some people may even avoid the situation all together. Stress can have physical consequences like sweating, a racing heartbeat, problems sleeping, and even headaches (Canadian Mental Health Association, 2017). It is important to avoid accumulating stress, which can lead to burnout, by practising some self-care. The human services field is exciting, emotional, and at times, overwhelming. In order to take care of others, you need to take care of yourself first.

TIME TO DEBRIEF

The fact that Matt was left alone during the incident with Geoff could have been a violation of his organization's policies and his profession's code of conduct. A **code of conduct** is a set of regulations and rules that dictate proper practice. Most professions have one. The child and youth care field has a code that encompasses taking responsibility for yourself, maintaining professional standards and conduct to adhere to professional practice, and maintaining both your physical and emotional wellbeing. It also includes a section that dictates that the child and youth care worker is responsible to their employer and the organization. This section states that workers must treat their colleagues with respect and professional consideration, acting in good faith (Ontario Association of Child and Youth Care, 2015). Matt's colleague did not intend to put him in harm's way; she made a different choice than Matt did for her own safety. (See the companion website for information on your provincial or territorial Child and Youth Care Association or the association affiliated with your professional designation.)

Another component that helped keep Matt safe were the techniques that he learned during his nonviolent crisis intervention training. Human services professionals who take this training learn how to reduce the risk of injury and promote safety for both themselves and the client (Crisis Prevention Institute, 2017). While his co-worker may have not followed the agency's protocol or the code of conduct for their profession, Matt had the training to keep himself and his client safe even though he was left alone.

KEY CONCEPTS

Code of conduct
Conflict of interest
Critical thinking development
Incident report
Individual Service Plan (ISP)
Moral philosophy
Safety plan
Self-care
Transitions
Trigger
Values

IN THE PURSUIT OF KNOWLEDGE

1. When a client is triggered, what are some things you can do to keep both them and yourself safe?
2. List the things you do for self-care.
3. What do you believe should be included in your profession's code of conduct?
4. If you were the supervisor, what would you say to Matt's colleague?
5. Please use the incident form template in the appendix and fill in the blanks as if you were Matt recording what happened.
6. Complete the values exercise on the companion website.

REFERENCES

Barber, K. (Ed.). (2005). *Oxford Canadian dictionary* (2nd ed.). New York: Oxford University Press. http://dx.doi.org/10.1093/acref/9780195418163.001.0001

Baxter, G., & Rarick, C. (1987). Education for the moral development of managers: Kohlberg's stages of moral development and integrative education. *Journal of Business Ethics, 6*(1), 243–248.

Brookfield, S. (1987). *Developing critical thinkers: Challenging adults to explore alternative ways of thinking and acting.* San Francisco: Jossey-Bass.

Canadian Child Care Federation. (2004). *HIV/AIDS and child care.* Retrieved from www.cccf-fcsge.ca/wp-content/uploads/RS_33-e.pdf

Canadian Mental Health Association. (2017). *Stress.* Retrieved from http://cmha.ca/documents/stress/

City of Toronto. (2015). *9-1-1 in any language.* Retrieved from http://911inanylanguage.ca/

Corsini, R. (1999). *The dictionary of psychology.* Philadelphia: Brunner/Mazel.

Crisis Prevention Institute. (2017). *CPI: Nonviolent crisis intervention.* Retrieved from www.crisisprevention.com/Specialties/Nonviolent-Crisis-Intervention

Elder, L., & Paul, R. (2010). *Critical thinking development: A stage theory.* Retrieved from www.criticalthinking.org/pages/critical-thinking-development-a-stage-theory/483

Family Support for Children with Disabilities. (2013). *Guidelines for developing an Individualized Services Plan (ISP) for specialized services.* Retrieved from www.humanservices.alberta.ca/documents/FSCD-ISP-Guidelines.pdf

Hare, R. (1981). *Moral thinking: Its levels, method and point.* New York: Oxford University Press.

Kenyon, P. (1999). *What would you do? An ethical case workbook for human service professionals.* Pacific Grove, CA: Brooks/Cole.

Kohlberg, L. (1969). Stage and sequence. In D. Goslin (Ed.), *Handbook of socialization theory and research* (pp. 347–480). Chicago: Rand McNally.

Kohlberg, L. (1976). Moral stages and moralization: The cognitive developmental approach. In T. Lickona (Ed.), *Moral development and behavior: Theory, research and social issues* (pp. 31–53). New York: Holt.

Ontario Association of Child and Youth Care. (2015). *Code of ethics*. Retrieved from http://www.oacyc.org/code-of-ethics

Piaget, J. (1932). *The moral judgment of the child*. Glencoe, IL: The Free Press.

Piaget, J., & Inhelder, B. (1969). *The psychology of the child*. New York: Basic Books.

Sheridan, P. (2016). Locke's moral philosophy. In E. Zalta (Ed.), *Stanford encyclopedia of philosophy*. Retrieved from https://plato.stanford.edu/entries/locke-moral/

OLIVE'S STORY

Hey, I'm Olive. I am a 25-year-old program facilitator at the Boys and Girls Club in my community. The Boys and Girls Club is a great place for elementary school children to hang out before school, after school, and on all of those non-instructional days, usually Fridays, when there is no school. We do all sorts of activities at the club and also go on field trips. My club also offers programming for school-aged children over the summer.

Walking school bus

Source: C. Genest

I do the walking school bus with the Boys and Girls Club. I pick up children in Grades 1 to 6. We walk from the elementary school down the street to the club. As the days go by, as the seasons change and the school year progresses, we discuss these changes during our walks. I noticed that these casual conversations were huge in the development of the children becoming friends. It is quite a walk, probably a good 15 to 20 minutes.

When we get to the Boys and Girls Club we either work as a group doing activities such as arts and crafts, or we play fun, cooperative games to build on the children's social and emotional skills. We provide snacks. The kids from the French school and the English school come and intermingle, and it doesn't matter to them what colour their skin is, what language they speak; you can really see through their body language and all of that what friendships are based on and how they are made.

The Boys and Girls Club is a really cool place to have all of that. Once we built a spaceship out of recyclable material. It was so cooperative! It did not matter what level they were at, everybody worked together. Yes, granted—sometimes people did not get along, and some children liked each other better than others, but I think that's all part of growing up and creating friendships.

One day on the walking school bus there were about ten kids. They were trying to figure each other out. Somebody said, "Oh, the sky is blue today." Somebody else, who was not having such a great day, turned around and said, "No, the sky is purple."

※

How would you react? You have two options:

Option 1: You respond, "No, it's not purple. Let's be logical." Turn to page 21.
Option 2: You respond, "It is a purplish shade of blue. Let's investigate."
Turn to page 23.

OPTION 1

There is a movement based on the bestselling book *How Full Is Your Bucket?* that encourages people to be positive towards one another. According to the authors of this book, almost every interaction with another person will be perceived as either positive or negative. "Each of us has an invisible bucket. It is constantly emptied or filled, depending on what others say or do to us. When our bucket is full, we feel great. When it's empty, we feel awful" (Rath & Clifton, 2009). In addition to a bucket, "each of us also has an invisible dipper. When we use that dipper to fill other people's buckets—by saying or doing things to increase their positive emotions—we also fill our own bucket. But when we use that dipper to dip from others' buckets—by saying or doing things that decrease their positive emotions—we diminish ourselves" (Rath & Clifton, 2009).

How do you think the child felt when they were told that the sky was not purple? Did that comment fill up their bucket or dip into it? This is more important to the developing child than the scientific fact that the sky is not purple. "We are not just intellects; we also have emotions, social needs, and bodies. Even if one's goal is only to improve academic outcomes, the best way to achieve that is probably not to focus narrowly on academics alone, but to also address children's emotional, social, and physical needs" (Diamond, 2014). What can you do to address the first child's emotional needs and make the other child aware of how their comment affected their peer? When you arrive at the club, you could start a discussion guided by **conflict resolution** skills and interpersonal communication principles such as **active listening techniques** and the use of **"I" statements**.

As you can probably imagine, sometimes conflict arises when working with people. It is important to assess every situation on its own since conflict can be functional or dysfunctional. It is functional if it improves decision making and increases energy; it is dysfunctional if it threatens group survival by destroying morale and trust. Everyone has a different conflict-management style that determines how they deal with conflict, engage with it, and in some cases, avoid it altogether. Every situation will be different; the important thing is to know that conflict may arise and to understand how you can manage it constructively. Here are a few tips for dealing with conflict (Bierman, 2013; Falikowski, 2013; Wood & Schweitzer, 2016):

1. Assess the situation. Does it have the potential to escalate? Do you need to intervene or can the individuals work it out themselves?
2. Find a good time and place to talk.
3. If it is a group conflict, be a mediator. Let both sides express their points of view without interruptions.
4. Focus on the problem, not the person. Use "I" statements. Instead of "You have done a terrible job," say "I am worried that we will get a bad mark on this."
5. Get all of the facts.
6. Provide a safe environment for everyone by employing active listening techniques such as looking at the person who is speaking, asking questions, and repeating what the speaker said.
7. Generate a variety of options to resolve the conflict.
8. Choose a solution that works for everyone involved.
9. Try the solution. If it does not work, go back and renegotiate.

Sometimes the conflict is a symptom or a trigger of a larger problem in the relationship. Perhaps there is an underlying problem in the individual's life. Maybe they were supposed to play soccer last night but the game was rained out. Ask questions, be engaged, show interest, and try to help the person recognize and express their feelings. As a role model, teach and demonstrate empathy while at work and in your everyday life by putting yourself in that person's shoes and seeing it from their perspective.

Loris Malaguzzi, the founder of the **Reggio Emilia approach** to early learning and child care, refers to the environment as the child's third teacher (Cagliari et al., 2016). Malaguzzi, as well as a lot of early childhood theorists who have influenced our philosophies and practices today, recognized that children need to be in touch with nature rather than being in care settings where the furnishings are all made out of plastic and painted in bright primary colours. Surrounding the children with a home-like atmosphere, with wooden tables and shelves, soft lighting, and pale natural colours such as green and blue, has a positive influence on their behaviour.

> In the study … the walls of the schoolroom were changed from orange and white to royal and light blue. A grey carpet was installed in place of an orange rug. Finally, the fluorescent lights and diffuser panels were replaced with full-spectrum lighting. As a result, Professor Wohlfarth reported, the children's mean systolic blood pressure dropped from 120 to 100, or nearly 17 percent. The children were also better behaved and more attentive, and less fidgety and aggressive, according to their teachers and independent observers. (Gruson, 1982)

It is important to bring the outside in but also to spend a lot of time enjoying the outdoors. These boys and girls are noticing a lot of changes in their world on their daily walk as the school year progresses. This helps them to develop an appreciation for their communities and the environment. That connection enables them to develop as citizens and become active participants in their communities.

OPTION 2: OLIVE'S CHOICE

> Try to realize that we all have good days and bad days, sometimes the sky is purple and sometimes it is blue, and sometimes what one little person might think happened at school may not have happened. Our walks were always interesting because that's when the conversations really broke out. Sometimes it was a group conversation and sometimes it was very individual. Sometimes it was a quiet walk because nobody had had such a great day, and it was just easier to walk and not say a word except to point out

different things. As the year went on the children got to know me, the adult, and I got to know their personalities, so I really got to see who was the funny one and who the more serious one, and who was more compassionate towards people. It was quite the mix of kids; Grade 1 to Grade 6 is a big age gap yet they always made sure that everybody was there before they left. If someone fell behind while walking, they made sure to let me know.

It is important for children in that age range to develop empathy towards others and see things from another's perspective. In order to do so, the children must first be able to recognize the feeling within themselves. It would be interesting to have the children reflect on what they are feeling by asking, "What colour is your sky today?" You could then give the younger ones choices, such as grey if they are having a not-so-good day, blue if they are having a good day, and orange or pink if they are having a great day. An exercise like this would also encourage them to recognize and express their feelings. You can discuss with the children what they could do once they get to the club if they are having a grey day. Suggestions might include going to a quiet corner to read a book by themselves, shooting some baskets out on the court, or eating a snack to see if it helps them to feel better. **Self-regulation** is an important practice that children can learn to help them overcome hurdles in their lives as they grow and develop, and it is essential for maintaining their own mental health. Dr. Stuart Shanker is a leader in Canada on this topic. "The ability to self-regulate refers to how smoothly a child is able to move up and down through different arousal states, which are critical for expending and restoring energy" (Shanker, 2013, p. 3). He refers to an arousal continuum ranging from inhibition, where at the lowest level the child is "hypoalert," "drowsy," then "asleep"; to activation, where at the highest level the child is "hyperalert" and then "flooded." The ideal is when the child is right in the middle, where they are "calmly focused and alert" (Shanker, 2013, p. 3). "When children are calmly focused and alert, they are best able to modulate their emotions; pay attention; ignore distractions; inhibit their impulses; assess the consequences of an action; understand what others are thinking and feeling and the effects of their own behaviours; or feel empathy for others" (Shanker, 2013, p. 3).

If you notice that a child is having a lot of grey days, you should change up your planning. "Almost any activity that requires focused attention, concentration, and working memory, and that also builds community, exercises the body, and brings joy, should be able to serve as the means for disciplining the mind and enhancing the skills needed for success in school and in life" (Diamond,

2014). You can put out some paint, brushes, and easels to encourage the children to express themselves through art. They could work together to create a mural or put on an art show for the community and auction off their masterpieces to raise money for the club. It is important to find the outlet that can help that child through a difficult time. Use your observational skills and casual conversations with the child—such as those you have during the walk, so they do not feel cornered or put on the spot—to determine what you can do to make them feel empowered and increase their self-esteem. What are their strengths?

Your program planning should be **strengths-based**. What do the children in your care need to develop as whole, healthy members of the community? What talents and abilities can each of them contribute? Your programming should be inclusive, engaging, and inviting so that the school-age children will want to participate. Often you will be more successful if you involve them in the planning and provide them with choices of activities or projects. It is important to take the time to research and write an activity plan before meeting with the participants. This will give you confidence and allow you to focus on the participants rather than the activity.

Planning can take many forms. For example, you can start with the ideal age of the participant; an observation that led to the creation of the activity; a list of the materials required to conduct the activity; an explanation of the invitation/provocation: the way you will invite the participants to come and engage in the activity. The procedure outlines how the activity will unfold, and the conclusion describes how you will end the experience. Be sure to take pictures and document what the participants say so you can create a learning story at the end to demonstrate to parents what you have been doing in your program.

> Learning stories can capture the intermingling of experience and disposition, the connections with the local environment that provide cues for further planning, the positioning of the assessment inside a learning journey, and the interdependence of the social, cognitive, and affective dimensions of learning experiences. At the same time, learning stories enable children and students to develop capacities for self-assessment and for reflecting on their learning. (Carr & Lee, 2013, p. 131)

You will also need to reflect on the experience and evaluate its strengths and weaknesses, and what you would change if you were to do it again. For example, maybe someone is interested in photography. You can start a photography club, or the kids can become junior reporters and make their own newspaper. Creating this atmosphere of teamwork and recognizing strengths in others helps to develop a culture of equality and respect, where each person is valued for what they can contribute to the team.

The programming you provide matters to the children, but do not forget about the environment. The children are also developing their observational skills. It is important for them to become objective observers of what is taking place around them. They might notice that someone is always being excluded from an activity. Once they have made the observation, they can decide what they are going to do about it. If, for example, one day they see a lot of garbage littering the sidewalk they can approach the city or the town and share their observations. Maybe they can ask that a garbage bin be placed in a certain location in order to reduce the amount of litter in the park. They can become activists for causes they believe in.

TIME TO DEBRIEF

Being an employee of an organization like the Boys and Girls Club, you have rules and regulations to follow for the safety of the participants. It is not always possible, for example, to pull two children aside to deal with a conflict when you have to be in ratio and are responsible for supervising more than two children. **Ratio** determines the number of adults needed to effectively supervise a certain number of children. On the walking school bus, there was one adult and ten children, thus a 1:10 ratio. Ratio is determined by the children's ages, recognizing that younger children require more supervision. For example, one adult can be assigned to care for a maximum of three infants, a 1:3 ratio. This rule is enforced by **licensing officers** and it differs from province to province to territory. The education of the employee also comes into play. Some employees cannot be left alone with children, according to that province's licensing regulations, if the employees do not have the necessary certification.

Working with people requires flexibility and the understanding that everyone has good days and bad days. A strengths-based approach enables a human services professional to focus on the good things and build upon them. The advantage of working for a licensed facility is that it helps to ensure that the employees can develop meaningful relationships with the children and provide them with quality care. It helps to create a safe environment and demonstrates to parents that the organization follows provincial legislation.

You need to ask the children to write their names on the sign-in sheet when they join the walking school bus after school and ensure that the parents sign them out when they come to pick them up at the club. As a staff member, you also need to sign in and out. When the licensing officer comes to visit, they look at the sign-in sheets to determine if ratio has been respected. You are required to have a copy of the child's registration form, including an emergency contact and a portable first aid kit, as well as telephone numbers for agencies such as the child abuse hotline. Licensing regulations for each province and territory list the items that employees need to carry in their backpacks when they are off-site. Employees and volunteers also need to have a valid, clear **criminal record check**, including the vulnerable sector.

KEY CONCEPTS

Active listening techniques
Conflict resolution
Criminal record check
"I" statement
Licensing officer
Ratio
Reggio Emilia approach
Self-regulation
Strengths-based

IN THE PURSUIT OF KNOWLEDGE

1. Take the VARK test on the companion website to determine your learning style.
2. Explore Dr. Shanker's website to examine the three key steps to self-regulation and reflect on what you can do to help children learn to self-regulate.
3. Sketch out what you think the ideal Boys and Girls clubhouse would look like. How would you furnish it? What would you put on the walls?
4. Plan an activity to do with the children in the after school program.

REFERENCES

Bierman, B. (2013). *Conflict management*. Retrieved from www.ofis.ca/wp-content/uploads/2013/07/Conflict-Resolution-Webinar-033111.pdf

Cagliari, P., Castagnetti, M., Giudici, C., Moss, P., Rinaldi, C., & Vecchi, V. (Eds.). (2016). *Loris Malaguzzi and the schools of Reggio Emilia*. London: Routledge.

Carr, M., & Lee, W. (2012). *Learning stories: Constructing learner identities in early education*. London: SAGE.

Diamond, A. (2014). Want to optimize executive functions and academic outcomes? Simple, just nourish the human spirit. *Minnesota Symposium on Child Psychology, 37*, 205–232. Retrieved from www.ncbi.nlm.nih.gov/pmc/articles/PMC4210770

Falikowski, A. (2012). *Human relations* (5th ed.). Toronto: Pearson.

Gruson, L. (1982, October 19). Color has a powerful effect on behavior, researchers assert. *The New York Times*. Retrieved from https://www.nytimes.com/1982/10/19/science/color-has-a-powerful-effect-on-behavior-researchers-assert.html

Rath, T., & Clifton, D. (2004). *How full is your bucket?* New York: Gallup.

Shanker, S. (2013). *Calm, alert and happy*. Toronto: Queen's Printer. Retrieved from www.edu.gov.on.ca/childcare/Shanker.pdf

Wood, J., & Schweitzer, A. (2016). *Everyday encounters* (5th ed.). Scarborough, ON: Nelson.

ALEX'S STORY

Hi! My name is Alex. I am a forty five–year-old family–school liaison worker, which is an awesome career. I work with elementary, junior high, and high school students by supporting their education and am responsible for providing their families with information and referrals to the programs and services available, such as Big Brothers and Big Sisters, where children are matched with an adult who can be their mentor. In my role, I am a dependable adult, someone who is consistent in the child's life, and someone that the child could turn to if they are seeking emotional support.

Mia

Source: C. Genest

Once a week I would meet with Mia for about an hour. We would talk about basketball. I did this to give her some female presence, to help her feel accepted as a girl. As far as I know, she had never known her mom. I'd been working with Mia for about a year when I began to have my suspicions that something must be going on at home. I didn't think she was being abused, but she kind of smelled, and I noticed that she was often wearing unclean clothing. I thought about it a lot because, in my line of work, sometimes when children come to school a little dirty, it's probably because their parents couldn't afford to do laundry or purchase new clothes. I asked Mia if she was showering regularly. Her response was a little weird; she said that when she had access to a shower she did. I thought it was weird because she lived in public housing, affordable housing with running water and electricity. Anyway, I dropped the subject and didn't ask any more questions for two more visits.

About three weeks later I decided to organize a pickup game of basketball in our gym. After the game, Mia asked if I could drop her off at home.
When I pulled up outside her building, her dad was waiting for her with
her little brother, sitting in a car full of garbage bags. I found this strange,
but I didn't think too much about it and went home. The next day at work
I noticed that Mia wasn't in the Grade 9 group's spring band performance
and her family wasn't present in the audience. I asked around and found out
that Mia's dad had taken her out of school, and some parents thought the
family was homeless. I found out that Mia was living with her dad and her
little brother in their car.

⚘

What would you do if you were in Alex's situation? You have two options:

Option 1: Call protective services: children cannot be homeless. If you choose
this option, turn to page 31.

Option 2: Don't call protective services. Her father withdrew her from school
so it is none of your business. If you choose this option, turn to
page 36.

OPTION 1

Homelessness is a complicated social issue that exists in every country in the
world. "Homelessness describes the situation of an individual or family without
stable, permanent, appropriate housing, or the immediate prospect, means, and
ability of acquiring it" (Canadian Observatory on Homelessness, 2017). There
are homeless people in every community who are living on the streets, living in
a temporary shelter, or couch surfing—moving from the home of one person to
that of another person, without having a specific home to call their own.

The majority of young people that I have interviewed describe themselves as
"street-involved," opposed to "homeless." Many of them who were living in
emergency shelters, couch surfing, or sleeping in bathhouses did not want to
be referred to as homeless, but rather street-involved. This is an important insight that tells us that the explanation of such a complex phenomenon, such

as homelessness, may not be fully captured in a definition. Perhaps a longer more sustained explanation or account that captures the fluid nature and ever-changing circumstances and chronic instability in which such youth often live, can reveal and explain what it means to be homeless, as well as provide direction for action. (Abramovich, 2015, p. 5)

Historically, when most Canadians thought about a homeless person, the image that came to mind was a single man who might have a mental illness or a substance abuse problem. But homelessness has become a crisis that affects everyone, including women, families, and youth (Gaetz, Dej, Richter, & Redman, 2016, p. 4). In 2016, there were 235,000 Canadians who experienced homelessness; 27.3% were women and 18.7% youths (unaccompanied by an adult). Indigenous people make up 28 to 34% of the people in shelters, and families are staying in shelters two times longer than individuals. The national occupancy rate (how full the shelters are) has increased by more than 10% since 2005 (Gaetz et al., 2016, p. 5). As mentioned above, 18.7% of all homeless Canadians are youths between the ages of 13 and 24. This means that, in the course of a year, approximately 40,000 Canadian youths experience homelessness. That is approximately 6,000 youths a night (Gaetz et al., 2016, p. 18). "Homelessness is a complex issue, and young Albertans who identify as sexual or gender minorities are at more risk of experiencing homelessness" (Government of Alberta, 2017). "Even though only 5-10% of the general population identifies as lesbian, gay, bisexual, transgender, queer, or questioning, as many as 25-40% of homeless youths identify as **LGBTQ2S+**" (Society for Safe Accommodations for Queer Edmonton Youth, 2017). "Research on homeless LGBTQ2S+ has identified the barriers the youth encounter stem from societal stigma, uninformed or less experienced service providers, and the fear of personal safety and/or rejection" (Burwick, Oddo, Durso, Friend, & Gates, 2014, p. 21). Alberta's youth plan "Supporting Healthy and Successful Transitions to Adulthood: A Plan to Prevent and Reduce Youth Homelessness" (Government of Alberta, 2017) has some great recommendations on how to support youth.

For the most part, social and economic factors contribute to the increase or decrease of the national occupancy rate. Historically, there were key Canadian initiatives where the government created mortgages that provided low interest rates; invested federal money into constructing more social housing that required low monthly payments based on the person's income; and created programs that subsidized rent payments for those who were not in social housing (Gaetz, 2010, p. 21). In 1999, the federal government launched the National Homelessness Initiative. This program encouraged community involvement. The National

Homelessness initiative is now called the **Homelessness Partnering Strategy**, and it provides assistance to communities across the country by providing funding and support for homeless individuals. The program was created as a result of **evidence-based practice** (Gaetz, 2010, p. 23).

In Canada, there are numerous different types of affordable housing programs and social housing programs created and maintained by the provincial and territorial governments. Each province and territory has responded differently to the homelessness crisis and coordinates its own strategies to end homelessness. Many communities have taken it upon themselves to create emergency shelters and coordinate supports for the homeless population. In some cases, the local police department assists in helping the homeless find supports in order to stay safe and warm in the winter. Often police officers also notice when someone goes missing (Gaetz, 2010, p. 24). There are three programs that are administered by the Canada Mortgage and Housing Corporation (2017). They are listed below:

1. The **Public Housing Program** is a project that targets low-income households that pay rent based on their income.
2. The **Non-Profit Housing Program** provides assistance to First Nations non-profit organizations that own and independently operate rental housing in urban areas.
3. The **Rent Supplement Program** helps households by setting a limited monthly rent based on a percentage of a family's income.

In our role as human services professionals, we help our clients find the best possible housing option. In order to do this, we need to research all the resources the community has in the way of supports for homeless individuals. Find out the organization's criteria for acceptance into their programs, whether there is a wait list, and how they process eligible applications.

One of the issues some of our clients encounter is the need for photo identification. In order to get photo i.d., they may need a birth certificate. This costs money, and your client may not know where they were born or exactly how old they are. Something as simple as not having the right identification can leave your clients on the streets. Find out the process, get the forms, and be ready for the day when you need to access the services. So much of our work is being an investigator, trying to figure out how you can help your client, and what you can do to put all the pieces together and come up with a solution.

Alex said that Mia was not going to school anymore. This could mean two things—either she dropped out (or her dad pulled her out) or she is being a truant. A **truant** is "a student who stays away from school without leave or explanation" (Barber, 2005). Canada has no federal department of education; this area falls under provincial and territorial jurisdictions (Kanevsky & Clelland, 2013). Primary and secondary education are compulsory in all provinces and territories between the ages of five or six and sixteen to eighteen, depending on the province or territory where the child is a registered student (Lehwald, 2014). It is important to note that homeschooling does not fall under this regulation. Homeschooled children are registered with an agency that provides curriculum and structure for the children under their charge, which means the children are registered students.

Some provinces fine the family each year for a child's truancy until the child reaches the age of voluntary withdrawal. Other provinces may have a truancy officer who works with the families and tries to encourage the child to attend class regularly. As a human services professional, you are required to know the regulations, processes, and legal documents for the school districts in your community so that you can explain to families the negative implications of skipping school. In some cases, truancy can lead to the removal of a child from the care of their parents.

Like education, protective services fall under provincial and territorial jurisdiction. Each province has its own system detailing how to respond to calls and how to investigate complaints. Working in the system is challenging because, as a protection worker, you are responsible for the lives of some of the most vulnerable children in Canada. As a family–school liaison worker, Alex needs to weigh Mia's vulnerability. Homelessness was putting Mia and her family at risk and could lead her to become a victim of human trafficking for the sex trade or domestic slavery, or a gang member. There is always the potential for Mia to find employment to help her family escape homelessness. Since she is vulnerable, you need to consider that she may explore illegal activities, and you need to encourage her to find employment in an industry that is supportive to youth. Often, the legal retail industry will provide discounts, scholarships, flexible scheduling, and opportunities for advancement. When working with an individual in similar circumstances, it is important to teach skills such as resume building, attending interviews, money handling, filling out government documents (for example, an application for a social insurance number), creating a budget, and filing taxes. These skills will help people throughout their lives.

If you have a concern, you have a duty to report it to protective services. In Prince Edward Island (2015), all islanders are bound by law to contact child protection services (that province's name for protective services) if they believe a child is being abused or neglected. The criteria includes suspicion that a child is being physically, emotionally, or sexually abused by a parent; suspicion that a child has been hurt and the parent could have prevented this but did not; and suspicion that domestic violence or neglect are occurring in the home.

Since you have decided to report Mia's family to social services, you would call their program, which is available 24 hours a day. Once the call is completed, the person who is assigned Mia as a client would open an investigation to determine whether her father failed to provide the **necessaries of life**. Why use the word "necessaries" instead of "necessities"? Because this is the word used in the Canadian legal system. According to section 215 (1) of the Criminal Code of Canada, parents, foster parents, guardians, and heads of families are under a legal duty

a) to provide necessaries of life for a child under the age of sixteen;
b) to provide necessaries of life to their spouse or common-law partner; and
c) to provide necessaries of life to a person under his charge if that person
    (i)   is unable, by reason of detention, age, illness, mental disorder, or other cause, to withdraw himself from that charge, and
    (ii) is unable to provide himself with necessaries of life. (R.S.C., 1985, c46, 215 (1))

In recent years, this has been a concern, especially in the province of Alberta, where parents and guardians have been criminally charged and tried in court for not providing the necessaries of life for the children in their care.

So how exactly are you going to make it work for Mia's family? Education is not as traditional as it once was, with students in school from 8:30 a.m. to 3:30 p.m., Monday to Friday. While this is still the norm with the majority of academic programming in most provinces and territories, there are also programs created specifically for students who do not fit the traditional model. We are all unique, and our strengths, developmental age, and abilities are different. Programs such as outreach schools provide students with the opportunity to learn in a flexible environment such as one-on-one instruction and evening classes. Virtual high schools provide an innovative programming option for rural students who do not have a plethora of courses readily available to them. These programs also help students with medical needs or elite athletes who cannot attend school on a regular basis, creating pathways for students to achieve their goals.

OPTION 2: ALEX'S CHOICE

> I didn't call protective services because there didn't seem to be any reper-
> cussions to the dad when other people reported him. I'm sure they did an
> investigation, but really nothing ever came of it. Dad passed it off as every-
> one else's issue and not his problem. I had no reason to believe that Mia's
> physical safety was ever in jeopardy; that was another thing that stopped me
> from going to the authorities. Mia never said anything to me about any type
> of abuse. She was never reluctant to give me a high five. I never saw bruises
> or anything. I had no reason to believe there were any issues. I just felt like
> reporting the case was going to cause things to get worse, and her dad said
> that they were moving soon. So the unwillingness of protective services to do
> anything coupled with the fact that Mia and her father were moving seemed
> reason enough for me not to push things further. I just wanted to be a positive
> role model for Mia rather than try to get more involved.

With the increases to the cost of living, some lower-income parents need to work extra hours to augment their income to be able to provide food and shelter (the necessaries of life) for their children. Sometimes this means they have more than one job. Longer working hours means more care for the children. Hiring someone to watch the children for a few hours a day or even an evening can become a costly option for families that are trying to get ahead. If a parent or guardian leaves a child unsupervised for a regular amount of time, or under the supervision of an older sibling under the age of twelve, the child is considered to be a **latchkey kid** (Rajalakshmi & Thanasekaran, 2015, p. 208). The term "latch-key" refers to the key that a child normally uses to enter the house when no one is home. It originated during in the 1940s while many fathers were off fighting in the war and many mothers were at work. This meant that children between the ages of five to fourteen were left by themselves after school until their mothers came home from work (Rajalakshmi & Thanasekaran, 2015, p. 208).

It is believed the effects of a being a latchkey child differ with age, but some of the most common effects are loneliness, fear, and boredom. Teenagers are more susceptible to drug and alcohol use, sexual promiscuity, and smoking (Rajalakshmi & Thanasekaran, 2015, p. 208). According to the Canada Safety Council (2015), the age at which a child can be left home alone varies across the country; usually it is below the age of ten. The council provides information for parents and guardians to determine if the child is prepared to be left alone along with an "on your own" home safety checklist. The Red Cross created a babysitter's course to help prepare children eleven and older by educating them and certifying them to look after younger children in a responsible manner. There are a lot of after-school care programs such as extracurricular sports teams, the Boys and Girls Club, and Out of School Care, so that children will have a safe and fun place to go that is supervised by adults and not have to shoulder the responsibility of being home by themselves.

Alex said that Mia was not going to school anymore. The United Nations Educational, Scientific and Cultural Organization (UNESCO) created a convention stating that children around the world have rights, including the right to an education. "The Convention on the Rights of the Child, ratified by 193 countries, is the most widely accepted human rights treaty" (UNESCO, 2017). In Canada there is no federal department of education; education falls under provincial and territorial jurisdictions (Kanevsky & Clelland, 2013). Primary and secondary education are compulsory in all provinces and territories between the age of five or six to sixteen and eighteen, depending on the province or territory where the child is a registered student (Lehwald, 2014). It is important to note that homeschooling does not fall under this regulation. Homeschooled children are registered with an agency that provides curriculum and structure for the children under their charge, which means that the children are registered students. Some provinces fine a family a certain amount each year if a child is truant until the child reaches the age of voluntary withdrawal. Others may have a truancy officer who works with the families to encourage the child attend class regularly. As a human services professional, it is important for you to know the regulations, processes, and legal documents of the school districts in your community and to be able to explain to a family the negative implications of not attending school. In some cases, it could lead to the removal of a child from the care of their parents. Many high schools are providing options to help increase the retention rate and keep students in school. Students with a high school diploma will have a higher income, on average, than students who have not graduated from high school (Alberta Education, 2016).

Like education, protective services fall under provincial and territorial jurisdiction. Each province has its own system for how it responds to calls and how it investigates complaints. Working in the system is challenging because, as a protection worker, you are responsible for the lives of some of the most vulnerable children in Canada. Many children who are removed from their homes are victims or have witnessed horrible abuses such as sexual, physical, and mental violence. Some are at risk of being trafficked into sexual exploitation rings and possibly used as drug runners, or at risk of becoming gang members. If you have a concern, you have a duty to report it to protective services. In Prince Edward Island (2015), all islanders are bound by law to contact child protection services (the province's name for protective services) if they believe a child is being abused or neglected. The criteria include suspicion that a child is being physically, emotionally, or sexually abused by a parent; suspicion that a child has been hurt and the parent could have prevented the harm but did not; and suspicion that domestic violence or neglect is occurring in the home.

TIME TO DEBRIEF

In this case, there really was no choice. While Alex is a seasoned human services professional, she still made a mistake. It is our obligation to report to protective services when we suspect that a child is homeless, is being abused, or is not having their necessaries of life met. Alex should have made the call; she really had no other choice.

KEY CONCEPTS

Evidence-based practice
Homelessness Partnering Strategy
Latchkey kid
LGBTQ2S+
Necessaries of life
Non-Profit Housing Program
Public Housing Program
Rent Supplement Program
Truant

IN THE PURSUIT OF KNOWLEDGE

1. Find out what the laws and process are for truancy in your community by locating the truancy regulation in the education act for your province or territory.
2. Think back to the people you knew in high school. What did your high school offer to keep them from falling through the cracks? What else could they have done to motivate students to graduate?
3. Quick case study: You are working with a homeless person trying to set him up with housing, and you realize that he needs photo i.d. He does not have any because someone stole his years ago. Years of drug abuse and mental health issues have caused some dementia and he does not know where he was born. What do you do? Who do you call?
4. What life skills did you learn growing up? How did you learn them? Is there something you wish you had learned but never did? What was it?

REFERENCES

Abramovich, A. (2015). *A focused response to prevent and end LGBTQ2S youth homelessness.* Retrieved from www.humanservices.alberta.ca/documents/abramovich-report.pdf

Alberta Education. (2016). *Why complete high school?* Retrieved from https://archive.education.alberta.ca/department/ipr/hsc/parent/why/

Barber, K. (Ed.). (2005). *Oxford Canadian dictionary* (2nd ed.). New York: Oxford University Press. http://dx.doi.org/10.1093/acref/9780195418163.001.0001

Burwick, A., Oddo, V., Durso, L., Friend, D., & Gates, G. (2014). *Identifying and serving LGBTQ youth: Case studies of runaway and homeless youth program grantees.* Retrieved from https://aspe.hhs.gov/system/files/pdf/76766/rpt_LGBTQ_RHY.pdf

Canada Mortgage and Housing Corporation. (2017). *Social housing programs.* Retrieved from www.cmhc-schl.gc.ca/en/inpr/afhoce/exsoho/exsoho_002.cfm

Canada Safety Council. (2015). *Preparation and Communication the key for children home alone.* Retrieved from https://canadasafetycouncil.org/preparation-and-communication-the-key-for-children-home-alone/

Canadian Observatory on Homelessness. (2017). *Canadian definition of homelessness.* Retrieved from www.homelesshub.ca/homelessdefinition

Criminal Code R.S.C. 1985, c. C-46, 215 (1). Retrieved from http://laws-lois.justice.gc.ca/eng/acts/C-46/page-51.html#h-74

Gaetz, S. (2010). The struggle to end homelessness in Canada: How we created the crisis, and how we can end it. *The Open Health Services and Policy Journal, 3*(1), 21–26.

Gaetz, S., Dej, E., Richter, T., & Redman, M. (2016). *The state of homelessness in Canada 2016.* Toronto: Canadian Observatory on Homelessness Press.

Government of Alberta. (2017). *Youth homelessness initiatives.* Retrieved from www.humanservices.alberta.ca/homelessness/youth-homelessness-initiatives.html

Government of Prince Edward Island. (2015). *Child protection.* Retrieved from www.princeedwardisland.ca/en/information/family-and-human-services/child-protection

Kanevsky, L., & Clelland, D. (2013). Accelerating gifted students in Canada. *Canadian Journal of Education, 36* (3), 231–259.

Lehwald, K. (2014). In search of right to free public education in Canada. *Education Law Journal. 24*(1), 25–47.

Rajalakshmi, J., & Thanasekaran, P. (2015). The effects and behaviours of home alone situation by latchkey children. *American Journal of Nursing Science, 4*(4): 207–211.

The Society for Safe Accommodations for Queer Edmonton Youth. (2017). Retrieved from www.safqey.com/

UNESCO. (2017). *Children's rights are human rights.* Retrieved from www.unesco.org/new/en/education/themes/strengthening-education-systems/early-childhood/single-view/news/childrens_rights_are_human_rights/

PAULETTE'S STORY

Hi! I'm Paulette. I have been a community youth worker for a family and community services association for ten years. In my role, it is my responsibility to work on developing relationships with families in order to help them make the best decisions to meet their needs and those of their children. I collaborate with the families on my caseload along with other service team members and service providers to develop a case plan to help the children and youth at risk as well as to support their families. It is my job to provide a strengths-based approach to managing services within a realistic timeline in order to mitigate any risk. I engage with families, help them understand their situation, and address the concerns that caused the children to be in need of assistance. In this position, I work with children, youth, families, and community supports to reduce the number of risks to the children and youth in order to help create a better life not only for them, but also for their families. I am also responsible for preparing parents and children for any court proceedings they may be involved in, and I help locate all the documents they need.

Mackenzie
Source: C. Genest

We were assigned a family. There were five kids. Mom was still at home, but dad had left very recently. The oldest child, Mackenzie, was twelve; the youngest was three. So we had quite a few children and mom was feeling the stress. The file came to us because Mackenzie was having a lot of anxiety about her dad leaving. She was the oldest, and now mom had to pay attention to four other children. Mackenzie decided that she was going to take off, run away. She was going to hide, go somewhere and stay there until midnight. Mom was at her wits' end, of course, because she had to take care of five children—some of them not yet in school—by herself, and try to figure out what to do with the oldest. She really wanted to bond with Mackenzie. She didn't want it to become a strained relationship, and she was trying to take care of herself as well. So there were a ton of factors going on.

What would you do if you were in Paulette's situation? You have two options:

Option 1: You were once a tween, let's start there. If you choose this option, turn to page 43.
Option 2: Off to family counselling we go. If you choose this option, turn to page 50.

OPTION 1: PAULETTE'S CHOICE

I came into the house, and they were very warm, very receptive people who really wanted the help. Actually, Mackenzie was fantastic. She recognized what she was doing. She was not unaware of why she was doing it. Mackenzie was much smarter than you'd think she would be at that age. She knew exactly what was happening, so she knew that the attention, even though it was negative, was getting her time with her mom, even though it was negative time. So we sat down. One meeting a week. And it actually only took a month. Sitting down with the twelve-year-old and saying, "Ok, what's going on? What's the deal? How are you feeling? How are things going?" and Mackenzie saying, "They are crappy, they suck. Dad's gone, I really like Dad." She didn't know why dad had left. There were marital issues but it wasn't a dangerous situation by any means. Mom and dad's relationship wasn't working out, so he had made the decision to pack up and go and didn't take the time to say goodbye. The younger ones were sure that their dad would come back, but Mackenzie knew he was gone. She was having a very hard time because she didn't get to talk to him. She felt the little ones were getting all the attention and she wasn't getting anything. "They steal my stuff. They come in my room. They play with my things. I get to sit here and be the oldest. I am supposed to help take care of them, and I don't want to," Mackenzie said. "I get to go out, and mom can worry about me for a while. Mom can worry about my problems and see how that goes."

So Mackenzie and I had some good discussions about what that was like. What was it looking like for her? What was she getting out of running away? I used the magic-scenario question. "If one day you woke up and everything was great and wonderful, what would that look like?" Of course, she said that dad would be home. That wasn't surprising. But she also said that she and her mom would have time together. So I said, "Ok, let's talk about that."

So we set up the meeting so that I could see mom half an hour before Mackenzie got home from school so that mom and I could debrief the last visit and sit and talk about what we were going to discuss that day so she would know where we were at. When Mackenzie arrived, mom just let us sit and visit in the kitchen.

One day, Mackenzie wanted to sit in her room. It was where she felt comfortable, so we sat there and visited. "Where are things at today? How did this last week go? What was better? What was worse? What was different? What was the same?" I asked. As we talked, we realized that the time she decided to take off was when she started boiling over. She was like this little tea kettle, you know? It was like a slow burn, but when it got there, it was explosive. I said, "Ok, so what can we do?" She said, "I need to calm down, but I don't know how."

I did some research and found a calm-down bottle. You take a water bottle, fill it about halfway with clear glue and halfway with water. Depending on how old the child is you can add more glue, and then you put glitter in the bottle. It is just a subtle thing, you shake it up. So I made a bottle and gave it to Mackenzie. I told her to shake it, shake the crap out of that thing. I said to get her anger out and then sit and just watch the glitter. I timed it. It took about ten minutes for the glitter to settle all the way to the bottom. While watching, I suggested she take some deep breaths in order to calm down. Then, after the glitter settled to the bottom of the bottle, I told Mackenzie to see where she was at, to take an inventory. She really, really liked that. She said afterwards that it was something that was hers too. She hid the bottle under her pillow. Mom knew that it was hers, so if the younger children took it, she would say, "No, that's not yours." Mom was very on board and supportive about taking it away from them.

The other thing we realized was that mother and daughter were having a really hard time communicating. They would get mad at each other and there was a lot of hurt. Those angry discussions that turned into yelling were never over one thing. During an argument, Mackenzie would bring up many things that had happened over the years. She brought up all these things with dad. She brought up all of the times that her mom didn't pay attention to her. Mackenzie would blow her top and scream at her mother, and mom was having a hard time not yelling back and telling her to go to her room. Dismissing the situation to try to diffuse it. So the three of us sat down together, and I said, "Ok, so this is the situation. I'm sensing a lot of hurt." They were so receptive, which was wonderful. They said yes, they both admitted it. It was a very mature conversation, awesome for a twelve-year-old to have. They realized that they were both hurting. This was not a fun situation for anyone.

I said, "I think what we need is a word that stops the conversation, like a pause button. It's not that we're going to stop yelling at each other and then come back and yell at each other in five minutes. It is a pause button that means, 'We are stopping right here, we are stopping because we know that we are blowing our tops. We both know that there is a line we are going over. It's too far, one of us is going to say something that is very hurtful. It is going to get worse and will become fuel for the next fire.' You can choose a word, I don't care what it is. You can talk about it before I come back next week. I don't care what the word is, it can be *zebra* for all I care."

So I came back the next week and asked what word they had picked. They said, "Zebra, we start laughing when we say it." So I asked, "Did you use the word?" and Mackenzie said, "Yes, we had to use it twice last week." It worked brilliantly because both of them were so on board with fixing the problem that they were ready for a solution. They had got to the point where they knew, and mom was so aware that she was going to say something hurtful—like don't be a brat or whatever—to dismiss those feelings. She knew this because she was already in that awful place, she knew her daughter was in the same awful place, and it was something that just had to stop. They couldn't keep doing this to each other, they had to be on the same page. Between finding ways to calm down and ways to communicate the fact that they were so ticked, they needed to take a break. It actually ended up that everybody was happy at that point, and we never got called back.

Often in human services, the need to interview members of a family in order to understand the family dynamic is imperative. We typically do this by creating genograms. Genograms are road maps to understanding a family; they are similar to family trees but include relationships and life circumstances. Simply stated, a **genogram** is a diagram of information about a family for at least three generations (Snapp, 2002, p. 25).

Paulette would draw a genogram for every family on her caseload. She probably works with up to fifty different families. She can bring the genogram on a family visit so she does not have to read the whole file to ensure that she is not relying on her memory while working with sensitive information. If she misplaces the genogram and someone finds it, most people will not understand what it means. A genogram can be drawn up during an interview with the family in a formal way, or it can be incorporated into an activity with the children and their parents and grandparents. Some social workers, counsellors, and child and youth care workers use the genogram as an art-based activity to help with the healing process.

There are three steps to creating a genogram. The first is mapping the structure of the family; the second is recording the information about the family, such as dates of births, marriages, and divorces; and the third is writing in the family relationships (McGoldrick & Gerson, 1985, p. 9).

The family structure is the basis of the genogram. It is a graphic that depicts how family members are legally and biologically related to one another from one generation to the next. The meaning is indicated by symbols. There are many symbols you can use to draw a genogram, but creating and adhering to an index of symbols can help lessen the confusion (McGoldrick & Gerson, 1985, p. 9). Regardless of the different ways people draw the symbols to represent each individual, there are some common symbols that are currently used (see Figure 1).

As you can see from the diagram, once a family structure has been drawn you can start adding information like family events and deaths. Draw a family in chronological order to help keep the history clear and easy to understand (McGoldrick & Gerson, 1985, p. 19). Show family relationships to help the human services worker understand the family dynamics (McGoldrick & Gerson, 1985, p. 21). See Figure 2 for more symbols. There are many more relationships and symbols not listed. Please refer to the companion website for great resources.

As you can see from the genograms, every individual has a place in the family—for example, the oldest child, the middle child, or the youngest. This is referred to as a person's **birth order**. Alfred Adler (1870–1937) was one of the primary theorists who believed that children in the same family do not have the same experiences and environment. Each child is born into a different psychological situation. It is not the actual order of the birth but the psychological situation the child is born into that is commonly referred to as the environment (Shulman & Mosak, 1977, p. 114).

The differences between sibling temperaments are prompted by different treatment by parents. This treatment is based on where the family is at emotionally and economically, and on the stability of the marriage (example: happy or unhappy) when the child enters the family. The different methods that the parents use to interact with their children will dictate how their personality traits will develop (Gilmore, 2016, p. 2). If the oldest sibling is developmentally delayed, the second child will demonstrate characteristics of a firstborn. Adler also

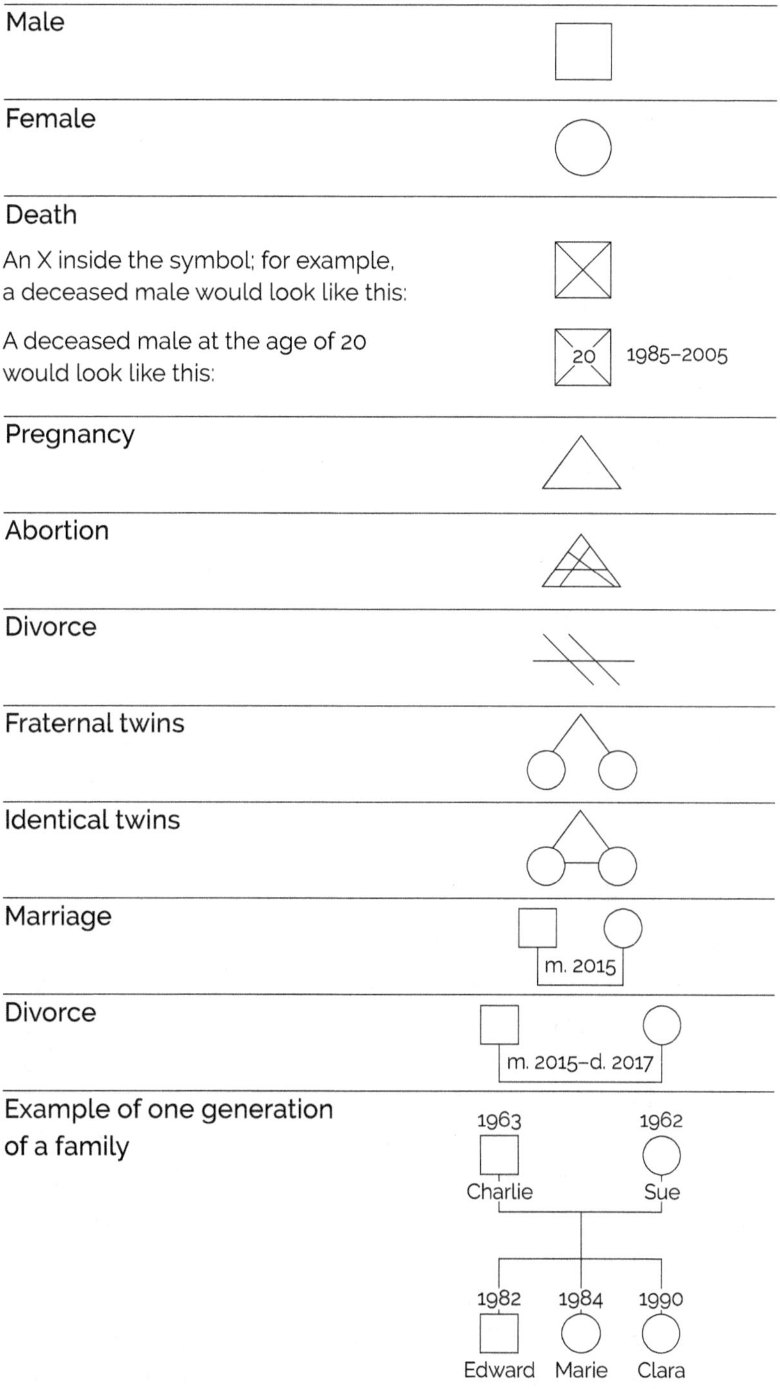

Male	□

Female	○

Death	
An X inside the symbol; for example, a deceased male would look like this:	⊠
A deceased male at the age of 20 would look like this:	⊠ 20 1985–2005

Pregnancy	△

Abortion	△

Divorce	

Fraternal twins	

Identical twins	

Marriage	□ ○ m. 2015

Divorce	□ ○ m. 2015–d. 2017

Example of one generation of a family

1963 □ Charlie   1962 ○ Sue

1982 □ Edward   1984 ○ Marie   1990 ○ Clara

Figure 1: Genogram

Source: Adapted from McGoldrick & Gerson, 1985

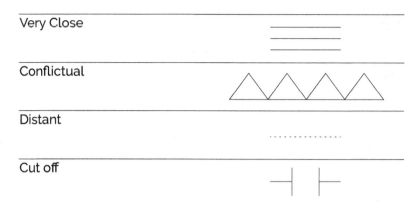

Very Close	
Conflictual	
Distant	
Cut off	

Figure 2: Genogram additional symbols

Source: Adapted from McGoldrick & Gerson, 1985

believed that the age gaps between siblings tend to increase or decrease the need for sibling rivalry (Shulman & Mosak, 1977, p. 114). What happens when the family changes? What if the children are the same but other people come and go? Or what if an only child becomes the middle child? The key is to know that a child's personality is fully developed around the age of six. It is the same with birth order. If a child is the firstborn in one family and then at the age of ten acquires older siblings, the child will still have the characteristics of an eldest child. A new stepbrother or sister who is older than the ten-year-old does not typically change their personality (Leman, 2009, p. 66).

Paulette and Mackenzie had some great conversations that really brought **attachment theory** into play. Attachment is "the emotional tie, experienced by an infant to a parent, from which the child derives security" (Boyd, Johnson, & Bee, 2018, p. 145). We know from John Bowlby's (1969) work on attachment theory that it begins in infancy with the mother, but what else does attachment mean? Human services providers need to understand the importance of attachment theory and the implications it may have in the lives of the children and youth with whom we work. For youth, when there is a breakdown of the parental relationship, it can become difficult for them to trust adults. Attachment can also affect the parent-child relationship because it has an impact on the quantity and quality of time the child has with each parent, whether the parents have shared custody or sole custody. If the child has siblings, he or she has to share the parents' time with the siblings.

As discussed by Dunn, relationships between siblings often provoke power struggles, competitiveness, and ambivalence (Dunn, 1988, p. 119). The term **sibling rivalry** is used often in society and is considered a universal phenomenon. Freud believed that siblings were rivals for their parents' love. This rivalry can be expressed through different reactions, from annoyance to rage, and it occurs early and often. Some families are unwilling to acknowledge the rivalry and do not admit it to others (Isaacs, 2016, p. 977). This can cause problems when interviewing children and working with families. An important element of our work is problem solving, and if we do not have all of the facts it becomes difficult to provide assistance. Often, sibling rivalry causes children to experience anger and depression, and can lead them to distance themselves from their parent. In Mackenzie's case, her mom will have less time to spend with her because she needs to care for the younger children and rebuild her life. This can affect Mackenzie's attachment to her mom and put Mackenzie at risk (King, 2002).

> The frequency and intensity of siblings' conflict, the risk of sibling bullying, and the associations with poor mental and physical health suggest greater attention to sibling interventions that reduce conflict and promote warmth is needed. Given that nearly 80% of children in the United States grow up with a sibling, and sibling relationships are one of the longest lasting relationships over a lifetime, it is important for researchers and clinicians to examine what interventions promote harmonious sibling relationships … There is a clear need for programmatic work aimed at sibling conflict and aggression because most parents want help with how to manage it, there is growing evidence for its negative effects for children's and adolescents' well-being, and it is the most common form of family violence. (Tucker & Finkelhor, 2015, p. 397)

Divorce can be difficult for everyone involved. For children, divorce can have both short-term consequences, which have a brief impact, and long-term consequences, which can last a lifetime.

The data on long-term consequences of divorce on children is conflicting. There are two camps. The pessimistic view is based on a longitudinal study by Wallerstein, Lewis, and Blakeslee (2000). In this study, they followed 131 children whose parents were divorced. The researchers found that when the children reached their 30s, they experienced more difficulties with interpersonal relationships.

Knowing about these results, Paulette can work with Mackenzie and her siblings to mitigate the long-term consequences of divorce. Otherwise, these consequences can influence the behaviour of the children later on, when they choose

Table 3: Negative effects of divorce on children

Long-term consequences	Short-term consequences
Pessimism	Anger
Worry	Depression
Self-deprecation	Anxiety
Increased risk of drug abuse	Health problems
	Change in social life
	Withdrawal
	Sadness

Source: Williams, Sawyer, & Wahlstrom, 2017

future spouses and become parents themselves. In order to break the pattern of unhealthy personal relationships, it is important to realize that children whose parents are divorced have had negative experiences in the past and this transition into a new phase of the relationship can be challenging for everyone involved. A great tip is to try to find a way to interact by doing something the child enjoys, such as going out for ice cream, to help make a connection and create an open line of communication. Paulette's decision to use the magic-scenario question, the calm-down bottle that the younger children were not allowed to touch, and the code word "zebra" gave Mackenzie and her mom strategies to use to restore the family's equilibrium and respect for each other.

As Paulette demonstrated, a little research can go a long way. Use your professional knowledge to repair relationships and establish a sense of belonging. Once the child knows you care about their wellbeing, a lot of great things can happen.

OPTION 2

By choosing this option, you will encourage the family to attend **family counselling**. It will benefit not only the twelve-year-old but her mother and the other siblings as well. Your role is to help find a family counsellor whose rates fall within the family's budget. There are a few areas that need to be explored. First, does mom have a benefit plan at work? If so, encourage her to contact her provider to see what they will cover. If she doesn't have coverage, does dad? Would he be willing to provide coverage through his plan? If neither parent has coverage, it is time for you to find a solution. There are provincial and territorial mental health agencies that provide free counselling for families and individuals. You do not need a referral. Just call the Mental Health intake line for your province or territory.

Family counselling usually starts with individuals in a case like this, given the wide range of ages of the children. The counsellor will meet with each person in the family, even the three-year-old. The family counsellor will provide recommendations, maybe even recommending that dad come to counselling. If this is the case, you need to talk to mom and decide who will reach out to dad, you or her. It is her choice, not yours. You will not be a part of the family counselling process, just the person facilitating the meetings.

While the family is pursuing counselling, do not forget that the twelve-year-old is putting herself at risk. To ensure her safety, you should meet with her. Sit down with Mackenzie and ask, "How can I help? How do you feel?" She is probably feeling abandoned, a common occurrence with children experiencing separation and divorce, trying to adjust to the changes in their relationships—in this case, with mom and dad. There has been a lot of research on the short-term and long-term effects of divorce on children's academic performance. But despite all of the research, not all children react the same way, and every situation is unique. Many children do feel sadness or anger, blame a parent or themselves, and experience a feeling of abandonment (McWhorter, 2005, p. 12). As a human services professional, it is your role to help this family adjust to their new normal. It is your job to determine the family's strengths and provide support and resources to help them move forward as a single-parent family.

The impact of divorce is different for every age group because their rate of maturity and development differ. It comes as no surprise that children's reactions change based on their **developmental age** rather than their actual age. The *Oxford Dictionary of Occupational Science and Occupational Therapy* defines developmental age as the "estimate of an individual's age based on achievement of developmental milestones" (Molineux, 2017). Sometimes preschool children regress developmentally; for example, children who were potty-trained suddenly start to wet themselves. School-aged children are often worried about their future, develop anxiety, and are at a higher risk for developing depression. Teenagers often take sides, develop negative feelings about the institution of marriage, and try to physically and emotionally distance themselves from home and family life. Gender also plays a role. Girls are more likely to seek connections with males and try to be perfect. Boys are more likely to try to fill their fathers' shoes in their mothers' lives. They often try to suppress their feelings and can become more aggressive (McWhorter, 2005, pp. 12–13).

How do you help Mackenzie? Together, you can create a plan that she is happy with, that makes her feel important. This is the beginning of the **case plan**. Participating in the creation of the case plan should help Mackenzie feel she has some control but also inform her about some of the risks she is taking. Where are some other places she can find a sense of belonging and be surrounded by positive influences? You can help the family connect with some great programs such as Big Brothers Big Sisters, family resource centres, youth groups, the Boys and Girls Club, and summer camps.

Depending on the family's needs, they may also qualify for respite through an agency such as Catholic Social Services. **Respite** is typically used to help families that have children with exceptionalities. Respite provides temporary care for the child in order to relieve the family from caregiving responsibilities for a brief period of time. Respite takes many different forms and can include care at home, a weekend at someone's home, or a day program. At home, the child will have a personal care worker to provide personal support (bathing), homemaking (cleaning), or professional care (nursing) in the comfort of their home. Stays away from the home in a facility or at a service provider's home take place over a short period of time such as a weekend but no longer than ninety days in a calendar year. Provincially and territorially, there are programs that provide daily respite care to help individuals who are high functioning but may need a safe place to go while their parents or guardians are at work (Queen's Printer for Ontario, 2017). Most individuals who use respite have some form of developmental, physical, or mental health problem that may make it unsafe for them to be left alone, and/or their needs may be so high that their family needs a break once in a while to avoid caregiver burnout.

Social determinants of health are the conditions in which individuals are born, develop, live, and age. They include the steps that are put in place to prevent and treat illness, as well as the distribution of resources and the power that is shaped by the political climate and society (Bell, Taylor, & Marmot, 2010, p. 471). All of these elements can be correlated with the six dimensions to wellbeing. In 1967, the World Health Organization defined an individual's overall wellbeing as not only the absence of physical illness but the state of physical, social, and mental wellbeing.

Wellness is determined by the various factors that are interrelated in order to provide a holistic approach to a person and their environment. It is about creating a balanced yet dynamic equilibrium. As a wellness advisor, one of the authors (Rothwell) promoted the six main areas of wellness as defined by Hettler (1980). They include social, emotional, physical, intellectual, spiritual, and occupational areas.

Social wellness emphasizes the individual and their relationship with others and their environment (Roscoe, 2009, p. 218). Emotional wellness is a continual process that includes a realistic self-assessment of the individual's approach to life, their mental health wellbeing, and their constructive expression (Roscoe, 2009, p. 218). Physical wellness covers everything from the person's physical health to their diet (Roscoe, 2009, p. 219). Intellectual wellness pertains to the person's ability to expand their knowledge and engage in creative and stimulating activities (Roscoe, 2009, p. 220). Spirituality is different for every individual. Spiritual wellness is the view that helps an individual to seek meaning and purpose in their existence (Roscoe, 2009, p. 220). Lastly, occupational wellness is the level of satisfaction or dissatisfaction an individual has with their job. It includes the contribution they can make to the workplace and provides them with a meaningful experience (Roscoe, 2009, p. 220).

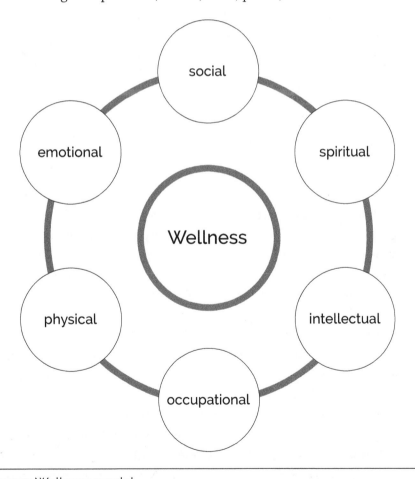

Figure 3: Wellness model

Source: Adapted from Hettler, 1980

Finances are often an issue for the families we work with, and the stress can affect many areas of wellness. Before the divorce, mom and dad probably had a joint account or joint investments. It is important that mom have a credit card and a bank account in her own name so she can establish her own credit score. If dad is not contributing financially, you might need to set them up with legal aid as the divorce proceedings occur and a decision is made regarding custody of the children.

There are also a lot of social services programs that include income subsidies for single-parent families. You need to become informed about the process in your province/territory and your community so you can provide the family with some viable options. Across Canada, there are a few programs available to low-income families such as subsidized daycare and before- and after-school care. If they qualify, the family will be responsible for paying only a small portion of the fees. Every province and territory also provides some sort of housing- or rent-assistance program. The best thing is to do your research in your community to help the families you work with, unfortunately though, there is often a long wait list for these services, so the sooner you get your client on the list, the better. Most provinces and territories also have specific programs to help families with children, which can diminish the wait time. There are also programs such as KidSport and Jumpstart that help lower-income families pay for the registration and equipment needed for their children to play organized sports such as hockey or soccer. Being involved in extracurricular activities is a great way for children to stay in shape and develop social, physical, and emotional wellness.

Some other ideas that may be helpful to the family include developing their skillsets—like creating a chart for chores so every child can contribute to the running of the household. The younger ones can vacuum, clean their rooms, and dust. The older ones can help do the laundry and make simple meals. As a human services professional, you might have to teach them these skills, along with meal planning on a budget, and provide them with information about how to access the closest food bank if necessary.

While we are concerned with the health of the family, in Canada the courts focus on the best interests of the children. In some situations the divorce may be amicable and the parents may decide on an agreement on their own. The Canadian Department of Justice (2015) recommends setting up a **parenting plan** that explains the parenting arrangement. A parenting plan covers the terms of the custody agreement and can include details such as pick up times, vacations, and what happens when a child is ill. Always remember to inform your clients that they have the duty to follow any court orders and written agreements.

TIME TO DEBRIEF

Consider Mackenzie and the feelings of abandonment that she is experiencing. We know from John Bowlby's (1969) work on attachment theory that it begins in infancy with a connection that develops between the baby and the mother, but what about the father? While Bowlby's theory was based on the mother, Lamb (1997) found that fathers play a significant role in the development of secure attachment in infants and toddlers that cannot be overlooked. Attachment is "the emotional tie, experienced by an infant, to a parent from which the child derives security" (Boyd et al., 2018, p. 145). Human services professionals need to understand the importance of attachment theory and the implications it may have in the lives of the children and youth. First, babies are resilient. This means they can often be comforted by numerous attachment figures (grandma, a babysitter, mom, or dad). When an infant is in a situation where they have extended visits with a noncustodial parent, they often do well. The change of environment and family members or guardians meeting the baby's needs does not necessarily have any long-term negative effects on their life if one person is replaced by another. Stern (1977) studied the interactions between carers and infants, their verbal conversations, and their facial expressions. It was his belief that, in the majority of cases, there is an intuitive component to these interactions in which the infant learns that the carer is available and that they can be understood and that the carer will respond to the cue (Ansbro, 2008, p. 235). According to Fonagy (2004), the method in which a caregiver responds to an infant is the method in which the baby starts to understand emotions, and they then go on to refine their meta-cognitive ability over the subsequent years (p. 186). Contemporary research on attachment confirms that early adverse experiences in a child's life are correlated with an increased chance of becoming an offender and experiencing mental health problems in the future (Ansbro, 2008, p. 234).

An important component of attachment theory is defined by Mary Ainsworth (1979). She created an experiment referred to as the "strange situation" experiment, which revealed the type of attachment an infant has to their care provider. It involved infants from twelve to eighteen months old. The infant and the care provider enter a room where there are some toys and a stranger. After some time, the care provider leaves the room. What is important, according to Ainsworth, is not what happens when the care provider leaves the room but what happens when they re-enter it (Ansbro, 2008, pp. 235–237). How does the infant react? Ainsworth categorized the infants' reactions into two styles of attachment: secure and insecure. Insecure attachments are either avoidant or ambivalent. A third type of attachment (an insecure type), called disorganized/ disoriented, was later added (Main & Soloman, 1986).

For older children, family trauma such as a separation or divorce may require additional support and time with the parent who is considered the "secure base." A **secure base** is a person to whom the child is attached (Ludolph, 2009, pp. 18–19). For youth like Mackenzie, the breakdown of the parental relationship can cause trust issues if her father was her secure base. Her father left, so she may find it difficult to trust other adults, and in many cases she will feel justified in not doing so. Breakups can also affect the parent-child relationship because the changes have an impact on the quantity and quality of time the child has to spend with their parents, especially when the breakup first occurs and the custodial parent is trying to make familial adjustments. In Mackenzie's case, her mom will have less time to spend with her because she needs to care for the younger children and rebuild her life, which can affect her relationship with Mackenzie and put the girl at risk (King, 2002). Being knowledgeable about the styles of attachment not only teaches us who we and others are but also how to approach a relationship in order to successfully work with our clients.

Table 4: Styles of attachment

Style	Definition
Secure	Positive attachment develops when a caregiver is consistent, attentive, loving. Characteristics: outgoing, can handle challenges, affectionate
Insecure	Scared or fearful, develops because the first bond with their caregiver was negative, sometimes even abusive. Characteristics: doesn't trust people or close relationships
Disorganized/disoriented	Complex, fostered by inconsistency. The caregiver's communication and attention are inconsistent and unpredictable. Characteristics: feels undeserving and in some situations unlovable

Source: Ansbro, 2008; Main & Soloman, 1986

KEY CONCEPTS

Attachment theory
Birth order
Case plan
Developmental age
Family counselling
Genogram
Parenting plan
Respite
Secure base
Sibling rivalry
Wellness

IN THE PURSUIT OF KNOWLEDGE

1. Find the symbols for transgender and adoption.
2. Create your own genogram.
3. What are some strategies that you could use to help a child open up and talk to you?
4. Research some programs that offer respite.
5. To create a case plan, what are some things that you would look for in order to work with this family?

REFERENCES

Ainsworth, M. S. (1979). Infant–mother attachment. *American Psychologist, 34*(10), 932–937. Retrieved from http://dx.doi.org/10.1037/0003-066X.34.10.932

Ansbro, M. (2008). Using attachment theory with offenders. *Probation Journal, 55*(3), 231–244.

Bell, R., Taylor, S., & Marmot, M. (2010). Global health governance: Commission of social determinants of health and the imperative for change. *The Journal of Law, Medicine & Ethics, 38*(3), 470–485.

Bowlby, J. (1969). *Attachment and loss: Volume I. Attachment.* New York: Basic Books. Retrieved from https://www.abebe.org.br/files/John-Bowlby-Attachment-Second-Edition-Attachment-and-Loss-Series-Vol-1-1983.pdf

Boyd, D., Johnson, P., & Bee, H. (2018). *Lifespan development* (6th Canadian ed.). Toronto: Pearson.

Canadian Department of Justice. (2015). *Create a parenting plan.* Retrieved from www.justice. gc.ca/eng/fl-df/parent/plan.html

Dunn, J. (1988). Annotation: Sibling influences on childhood development. *Journal of Child Psychology and Psychiatry and Allied Disciplines, 29*(2), 46–57.

Fonagy, P. (2004). Early-life trauma and the psychogenesis and prevention of violence. *Annals of the New York Academy of Sciences, 1036*(1), 181–200.

Gilmore, G. (2016). Understanding birth order: A within-family analysis of birth order effects. *Undergraduate Journal of Humanistic Studies, Spring*(3), 1–8.

Hettler, B. (1980). Wellness promotion on a university campus. *Family and Community Health, 3*(1), 77–95.

Isaacs, D. (2016). Editorial: Sibling rivalry. *Journal of Paediatrics and Child Health, 52*(11), 977–978.

King, B. (2002). Parental divorce and interpersonal trust in adult offspring. *Journal of Marriage and Family, 64*(1), 642–656.

Lamb, M. (1997). Fathers and child development: An introductory overview and guide. In M. E. Lamb (Ed.), *The role of the father in child development* (3rd ed., pp. 1–18). New York: John Wiley & Sons, Inc.

Leman, K. (2009). *The birth order book: Why you are the way you are.* Grand Rapids, MI: Revell.

Ludolph, P. (2009). Answered and unanswered questions in attachment theory with implications for children of divorce. *Journal of Child Custody, 6*(1), 8–24.

Main, M., & Solomon, J. (1986). Discovery of a new, insecure-disorganized/disoriented attachment pattern. In T. B. Brazelton, & M. Yogman (Eds.), *Affective development in infancy* (pp. 95–124). Norwood, NJ: Ablex.

McGoldrick, M., & Gerson, R. (1985). *Genograms in family assessment.* New York: W.W. Norton & Company.

McWhorter Sember, B. (2005). *How to parent with your ex.* Naperville, IL: Sphinx Publishing.

Molineux, M. (2017). *Oxford dictionary of occupational science and occupational therapy.* New York: Oxford University Press. Retrieved from www.oxfordreference.com/view/10.1093/acref/ 9780191773624.001.0001/acref-9780191773624-e-0163?rskey=i4RHcq&result=1

Queen's Printer for Ontario. (2017). *Respite care.* Retrieved from www.ontario.ca/page/ respite-care

Roscoe, L. (2009). Wellness: A review of theory and measurement for counselors. *Journal of Counseling & Development, 87*(2), 216-226.

Shulman, B., & Mosak, H. (1977). Birth order and ordinal position: Two Adlerian views. *Journal of Individual Psychology, 33*(1), 114.

Snapp, R. (2002). Genograms: Charting your connections. *Journal of Christian Nursing, 19*(4), 25.

Stern, D. (1977). *The first relationship: Mother and infant.* Cambridge, MA: Harvard University Press.

Tucker, C., & Finkelhor, D. (2015). The state of interventions for sibling conflict and aggression: A systematic review. *Trauma, Violence, & Abuse, 18*(4), 396–406. Retrieved from http://dx.doi.org/10.1177/1524838015622438

Wallerstein, J., Lewis, J., & Blakeslee, S. (2000). *The unexpected legacy of divorce: A 25-year landmark study.* New York: Library of Congress.

Williams, B., Sawyer, S., & Wahlstrom, C. (2017). *Marriages, families, and intimate relationships* (4th ed.). Englewood Cliffs, NJ: Pearson.

Wood, J., & Schweitzer, A. (2016). *Everyday encounter*s (5th ed.). Scarborough, ON: Nelson.

World Health Organization. (n.d.). *Frequently asked questions.* Retrieved from www.who.int/suggestions/faq/en/

PHOUNG'S STORY

Hi! I'm Phoung. I was a group-home personal support worker for eight years. I was responsible for the safety and wellbeing of all of the children in the group home. I worked with the children to ensure that the general housekeeping was done, that they attended to their personal hygiene, went to school, and took their medication on time, and I transported them to and from appointments. I helped prepare meals and planned activities to do with the children after school and on weekends. My shifts ranged from days to evenings and even some nights, and my duties changed based on when I was scheduled to work.

Colleen

Source: C. Genest

When I first started I was young and thought I was changing the world. I was working with this one girl, Colleen. She had a really, really rough life. She had psychosis, I'm not sure what kind of psychosis, but I think it was probably schizophrenia. Anyway, I got really close to her really quick, and she told me things she wouldn't tell anyone else. She trusted me. She didn't trust anyone because she had lived in foster care since she was two. They had found her abandoned in a run-down house that was completely disgusting, and she was placed in foster care. She came to the group home when she was in her early teen years. I am a sucker and it just broke my heart, so I got close to her. She would see things. She would hallucinate a lot and take her anger out on everyone except me. It went right to my head. I thought I had changed her life. You know, it got me feeling like I was doing something great with her. Every day I would come home just pumped because I thought I was making breakthroughs with her and it was just an awesome feeling.

We would play with dolls, and we would play games. We watched *Harry Potter*. She loved Harry Potter. She had an imaginary friend named Cynthia who would tell Colleen to do bad things. Sometimes she would look up and tap her foot, and you'd know that Cynthia was there telling her to do bad things. When she was looking down at the floor, it was Harry Potter and Dumbledore flying around down there. They were good. You'd know what kind of mood she was in by where she was looking.

Colleen was overweight. She was on a strict diet. I was a little relaxed about it, and if I was in the kitchen I'd sneak her a little piece of something. She has to have a fun life. Yes, she was in a group home and there are strict rules, but you also have to live a little. Although I know kids with mental illness need majorly strict routines, it was also nice to treat her a little too.

⚘

What would you do if you were in Phoung's situation?

Option 1: She likes me! I'm making a difference. If you choose to continue relaxing the rules when working with Colleen, please turn to page 63.
Option 2: Not everyone is going to like me, that's ok! If you choose to follow Colleen's strict routines, please turn to page 69.

OPTION 1: PHOUNG'S CHOICE

Until one day Colleen did get mad at me. She came at me and she threw things at me and she called me every name in the book. My heart broke because I thought, you know, I felt that everything I had done with her had gone out the window. I took it personally and I was crushed. Everyone used to put me down about how close she and I were. They said that she didn't take me seriously. That I was just her friend and a playmate, that she didn't respect me. After that, they all got me to be strict with her, and it was miserable. My job was miserable, it was awful. But after that major incident I completely stopped, and she was really mad at me. She was really, really mad at me, so we didn't have a good relationship at all. So that was my worst day when she attacked me, it was more the verbal attack that crushed me, I thought it was all me, it wasn't her. It was my expectations. It was about how I thought I was doing so great. These people need someone in this world to go to bat for them. I used to tell her all the time that I wished I could take her mental illness away. She was always saying, I wish my brain would just work. She did know. She was so frustrated with herself. It was the only thing that made that job worthwhile.

In the human services field, we work with a variety of people. It is easier to establish connections with people and work for organizations that share our interests and enrich our lives. It is important to understand the breadth of the field because there are many different areas under the umbrella of human services. They include but are not limited to rehabilitation, residential child and youth care, juvenile justice, school-based child and youth care, hospital-based child and youth care, early learning and child care, early intervention, community-based child and youth care, parental educational and support, and recreation. When choosing an area to explore, do not forget to consider your own comfort level and strengths and to take into consideration what part of the field interests you at the time. It is not uncommon to change jobs and positions as you move through your career.

Phoung thought that she was being a professional by getting to know her client and doing what she could to make her happy. She felt sorry for the girl and her situation. It is important to remember that, while you can have empathy for the client, you are an employee of an organization. Not only do you need to follow the code of ethics of your profession, you also need to follow the policies and procedures of the organization. Before applying for a job, do some research about the organization to see if it shares your values and philosophy. It is important that you advocate for your client, but it will not be a good fit if you are undermining the decisions and policies of your employer because you do not agree with them. According to Wallace (1972), policy is considered a plan of action that is usually created by the staff of the organization or agency, and the policy is then presented to a board of directors for review (p. 1017).

Most organizations and agencies will have some guidelines or policies in a **staff handbook**. In most of the handbooks you will find information about dress codes, protocols for taking a sick day, how to handle client emergencies—really, everything you need to know about your position. Your employer should also provide you with a job fact sheet or an employee expectation list. This information will be used during a review of your performance as an employee.

When you are hired as a staff member, you are on probation. This probationary period can last up to several months depending on whether you are working full time or part time. This period is a time for you and your employer to see if you are a good fit for the job. At the end of this probationary period, you will meet with your supervisor for a performance review. You will discuss your strengths and plans for professional development to improve your performance. At this time, the employer will decide either to extend your probationary period, hire you on as a permanent employee, or terminate your employment. The labour laws for each province and territory clearly state the circumstances pertaining to the termination of an employee and what you need to do if you want to resign from your job.

Table 5: Labour laws by province/territory

Province/Territory	Labour laws/Provincial assistance or departments
Alberta	Provincial department known as Alberta Labour Employment Standards Code
British Columbia	Provincial department has an Employment Standards branch. Employment Standards Act and Regulations
Manitoba	Department of Growth, Enterprise and Trade. Has Employment Standards documents that employees can consult to learn about their workplace rights. Employment Standards Code
New Brunswick	Department of Post-secondary Education, Training and Labour Employment Standards Act Employment Standards Act Regulations
Newfoundland and Labrador	Department of Advanced Education, Skills and Labour Labour Standards Act
Northwest Territories	Department of Education, Culture and Employment Employment Standards Act and Regulations
Nova Scotia	Department of Labour and Advanced Education. Discusses the Labour Standards legislation and provides assistance to Nova Scotians. Labour Standards Code
Nunavut	Labour Standards Act

continued

Province/Territory	Labour laws/Provincial assistance or departments
Ontario	Ministry of Labour provides Employment Standards documents Employment Standards Act, 2000 Employment Protection for Foreign Nationals Act, 2009 Pay Equity Act Protecting Child Performers Act, 2015
Prince Edward Island	Department of Justice and Public Safety Employment Standards Act
Québec	Department of Employment and Labour Act respecting the Ministère du Travail (Chapter M-32.2)
Saskatchewan	Government of Saskatchewan The Saskatchewan Employment Act
Yukon	Department of Community Standards Employment Standards Act
Federal	Canada Labour Standards Regulation C.R.C., c. 986 Canada Occupational Health and Safety Regulations (SOR/86-304). Canada Labour Code R.S.C., 1985, L-2

In most cases, many of the issues that you will encounter will be discussed at staff meetings and can be addressed with the rest of your team. If you have a question, now is the time to ask it. It was probably at a staff meeting that the team decided to implement the system to address Colleen's caloric intake. If, after some discussion, the majority decides to implement the system, you must follow their lead, even if you do not agree. After trying the system for a month, you can bring the matter back up at a staff meeting for analysis. Is the behavioural strategy effective? What are the challenges? If it is not working, is there something else you can try?

Due to the fact that there are many employees who come into contact with each client, some organizations have a **communication book**. After your shift, you record in the communication book any important information that you believe needs to be passed on to the other members of the team, both immediate, such as your coworkers, and external, such as social workers, caseworkers, and probation officers. Before your shift, it is important to read the information in the communication book to make sure that you are up to date with what has been happening. The communication book is a great way to ensure that all of the team members are on the same page. As Phoung pointed out, for vulnerable individuals, consistency of care is important and the communication book is one tool that can keep everyone informed and on the same page. Since it is a written document, it can be used as evidence outside of your organization, therefore it is essential that you remain professional and use objective language. Using **objective language** means recording factual information. You need to report exactly what you saw and heard so that someone who reads your report can see what you saw and hear what you heard in order to make a decision, without being influenced by your choice of words. You remain objective by removing all emotion from your writing. Be sure to record the date and time, and include a lot of details such as, "C was standing in front of the bedroom window with her arms crossed in front of her, looking straight ahead." Report only the facts and respect confidentiality in case the book is lost or the information is needed by another agency.

When you are in a helping relationship, it is important to understand that you need to listen and explore the issues and problems that your client is encountering, but as human services professionals, we are not counsellors. **Counselling** entails a formalized relationship that is based on a specific set of traditions and practices. It is a process conducted with a client in a stressful and challenging relationship (Srebalus & Brown, 2000). Counsellors have two specific goals: to help the client manage a problem and to look at their general ability to manage problems and develop opportunities. A good candidate to be a counsellor is someone who has integrity and is objective. If Phoung is interested, she should be encouraged to go back to school to become a counsellor.

A lot of people may not have picked up on Phoung's **observational skills**. Do you remember what it meant when Colleen was looking up or down? Those are very slight physical behaviours that a lot of people may not have noticed, but they actually meant a lot to Colleen. Observation is a skillset that helps all human services professionals better understand and analyze a situation because they are able to watch closely and take in their surroundings. Observation can help you figure out your clients' possible triggers. Maybe you observed that every time your client comes home from school she is depressed; could that mean she is being bullied? What about observing the way your client interacts with adults, other youth, or even what kind of music she likes? Put all of these little observations together to get a better idea of what your client is experiencing. It can help explain a client's behaviour, what they think or feel, and what they hope for or fear. A lot of people do not use their verbal communication skills to explain what is happening because they do not have the skillset or they simply do not want to. A way to observe a client is to take notice of their general state of wellbeing. Are they anxious or uncomfortable? What is their body language telling you and what are you hearing? Record your observations in the communication book or share them at a staff meeting in order to have a better picture of your client as an individual and to enable you to better meet their needs.

The method with which we choose to communicate will help us work effectively with our clients and other staff members. We work with individuals with varying levels of education, community members from around the globe, and people who may be nonverbal. We use both verbal and nonverbal communication to express a message and a meaning that we want others to understand. Language is abstract; it is based on manipulation of symbols (Schneider, 2009, p. 523). Symbols are ambiguous and arbitrary; they are representations of a phenomenon in our social world. As human services professionals, we recognize the importance of symbols in language; we think of the language and symbolic representations found in art and music. A child or an adult can tell us their life story based on the picture they draw. What if it is easier for a person to express a situation or a feeling by using art, dance, or music instead of words? Communication does not need to occur verbally. Tattoos, for example, are a method of representing thoughts and beliefs and convey a message. In 2008, the Canada Border Services Agency Organized Crime Section released *Tattoos and Their Meanings* to assist officers with the identification of gangs and organized crime members. Knowing and recognizing symbols can help you identify the needs of a client. It can also help you understand a person's background and belief system.

As discussed by Wood and Schweitzer (2016), verbal and nonverbal communication have similarities; they are rule-guided, symbolic (intentionally or not), and they reflect culture (p. 161). Communication between two people or groups of people helps an individual to form their personality and provides an opportunity for the transmission of a person's social experience (Preja, 2013, p. 240). You can tell a lot about what a person is thinking and feeling based on their nonverbal communication. Their thoughts and feelings show in their reaction and emotional response to a situation. Nonverbal communication is often learned behaviour and a form of self-contained communication (Preja, 2013, p. 239). When a person is smiling, we associate that with happiness. If you are constantly checking your phone when you are talking to a client, you are communicating disinterest. Put away your phone. All communication has a social context and relevance. We communicate our feelings and our messages not only with words but also by the way we stand and how we behave.

OPTION 2

Although it is not always easy, it is important for human services professionals to see the bigger picture and have respect for the client and their needs as
well as the rules and regulations of the organization. You can have empathy
for the client and may sometimes want to bend the rules or alter the treatment plan in order to please them, but it is not necessarily in the client's best
interests. It may cause some resentment among your colleagues if they have to
deal with the consequences when you do not adhere to the plan. Teamwork
involves having everyone on the same page. Several studies conducted by the
Harvard Business Review revealed that, in addition to J. Richard Hackman's
three conditions—"a compelling direction, a strong structure, and a supportive
context" (Haas & Mortensen, 2016, para. 2)—teams today benefit if they have
"a shared mindset ... a common identity and common understanding" (Haas &
Mortensen, 2016, para. 16). You are not there to be liked by the client but to
do what is best for them according to the team of experts.

Before we move on, it is important to understand that Colleen's situation is
not unique. Many of our clients will experience some form of mental health issue
and thousands of our clients experience poverty and homelessness. According to
Statistics Canada, in 2014 the percentage of Canadian children (under the age
of 18) living below the poverty line was 14.7%, and the percentage of children in
"female lone-parent families" living below the poverty line was 44.9% (Statistics
Canada, 2017). The **poverty line** typically refers to the lowest cut-off point for
gross income (taxable earnings). It is the amount of money an adult will need to
earn to purchase the necessities of life such as food, shelter, and clothing. Anyone
earning less than this would fall below the line and be considered to be living in
poverty (Statistics Canada, 2015). In Canada, the low-income cut-off (LICO)
is $18,421 for a single person, $22,420 for a two-person household, $27,918 for
three people, and $34,829 for a four-person household (Statistics Canada, 2015).
As we see in this story, Colleen's circumstances meant that she was living below
the poverty line. She lived in unsanitary and unsafe conditions until the age
of two, which put her early development and mental health wellbeing at risk.
Within the womb, the fetus is dependent on the mother's physical health. If the
fetus is exposed to **teratogens**—factors such as poor diet, chronic illness, mental
illness, alcohol, smoking, and drugs—their brain development can be adversely
affected (Boyd et al., 2018, pp. 74–75).

Mental illness is common among children and youth. It is believed that in
the province of British Columbia one in seven young people will experience a

mental illness at some point during their childhood (Canadian Mental Health Association British Columbia, 2014). According to the Canadian Mental Health Association, British Columbia Division (2014), if a mental illness is not treated early, it can affect the person for the remainder of their lives (p. 1). Some common mental health disorders in youth include **anxiety disorders, attention deficit hyperactivity disorder (ADHD), eating disorders, conduct disorders, mood disorders, substance abuse,** and **depression**. Some individuals may experience a **psychotic disorder,** but these are rare (CMHABC, 2014, p. 2). There are many different types of anxiety disorders, but they share the characteristic of an excessive fear of things and situations, both real and imagined.

Attention deficit hyperactivity disorder (ADHD, or ADD if there is no hyperactivity) is among the most prevalent behavioural disorders in children. It is a brain disorder that causes a pattern of hyperactivity, inattention, and impulsivity that interferes with the child's ability to function and affects their development (National Institute of Mental Health, 2017a). Eating disorders include anorexia, bulimia, and binge-eating. They are associated with a wide range of adverse physical, psychological, and social consequences. Individuals with eating disorders are concerned and often extremely distressed about the appearance of their body and make an effort to manage their weight by controlling their food intake (CMHABC, 2014). Conduct disorders involve aggressive, disruptive, and, at times, hostile behaviour that is considered not appropriate for the child's age. The child may not heed the rules and can be destructive towards people or property (CMHABC, 2014). Psychosis is the state in which a person loses touch with reality. An individual who has a psychotic disorder could have unusual or bizarre experiences that they believe to be real. Often they will experience auditory or visual hallucinations and can exhibit abnormal behaviours (National Institute of Mental Health, 2017b).

It is important to become educated about all of the mental illnesses and learn about the strategies you can use to work with clients who have been diagnosed with one of the above conditions. Be sure to consult the client's case plan and find out about the course of action the agency you work for has in place to help the client. The client might also be on medication as a result of a diagnosis to help control the symptoms and give them a better quality of life. As human services professionals, we do not have the ability to prescribe medication or even give recommendations concerning prescriptions. That being said, with permission we can administer medication and securely store and manage the medication of the clients in our care.

There are different types of medication. Over-the-counter medication does not require a prescription. Normally used for short-term relief of pain, fever, teething, or cramps, it can be found on the shelves of a pharmacy and includes cough and cold medications, painkillers, vitamins, and medicated creams. Before administering a new medication to children under the age of two, you should consult a medical professional. When giving medication to older children, always follow the instructions on the back of the box for recommended dosage. Record the date, time, and amount of medication administered and check regularly for adverse reactions, such as a rash or swelling (Pimento & Kernested, 2015, pp. 200–201).

The other common type of medication that you will be working with is available only with a prescription from a doctor or medical professional. It is extremely important that this medication be stored in its original container with the client's name on the label as well as the name of the medication and dosage instructions. Follow the instructions on the bottle, and if you ever have any questions you can always call a pharmacist. Whether the medication is prescribed or not, it is important that you follow the protocol at your agency in order to act responsibly and avoid medication administration errors (Pimento & Kernested, 2015, p. 202). As described by Pimento and Kernested (2015), the general protocol for administering medication is as follows:

1. If you are working with families in a daycare setting, or at a day program for adults or children and the family is involved, make sure you have the parent or guardian sign a consent form that includes the client's name and date, the name of the medication, the reason for taking it, the dosage, the number of times a day it needs to be administered, and the date and time it was last taken.
2. If it is for a client in care, follow the instructions provided by the doctor or medical professional.
3. In both cases, keep all medication in a locked area not accessible to the clients. Any liquid medication should be stored in a locked container in the fridge.
4. Know who is responsible for administering the medication during the shift. Any confusion can lead to medication mistakes that can have serious consequences.
5. Prescription labels must include the client's name, the name of the medication, the dosage, the number of times a day it should be taken, and how it is administered. The pharmacist will typically include instructions that state "Take with food," for example.
6. Keep detailed records indicating when you administered the medication and the dose given. This can help other workers and could possibly save the client's life. (p. 202)

It is important to know your client's medical history, including allergies! Have they been prescribed epinephrine because they develop an allergic reaction to a specific food, bee sting, or medication? Do they smoke cigarettes? Do they take multivitamins? Sometimes the interaction between substances diminishes the effectiveness of the medication or causes negative side effects. This information can change. Stay informed! It is your role as a professional to find out what your organization's policies are pertaining to the administration of medication. Some agencies have nurses on-site who will provide the medication to the clients and others do not. If you have concerns about the safety of the client, you can document your concerns and inform your supervisor.

In Cowan's story (p. 91), there will be information on alternative therapies that can be used in conjunction with medication that is prescribed or not. **Naturopathy** uses both biomedical and natural forms of medicine. Naturopathy is believed to stimulate the healing powers of the body and treat the underlying causes of a disease. The treatments are chosen based on the individual's spiritual beliefs, psychological wellbeing, and social wellbeing, as well as their environmental factors. In order to subscribe to this form of medicine, a client will need a lifestyle change, make use of natural therapies, acupuncture, and homeopathy, and will follow a strict diet (Canadian Association of Naturopathic Doctors, 2016). There are three main types of individuals who use naturopathy:

1. The individual is proactive, looking for health promotion strategies and disease prevention.
2. The individual has a range of symptoms that they have not been able to address on their own or with a biomedical professional.
3. The individual has been diagnosed with an illness and is looking for an alternative treatment. (CAND, 2016)

Increasingly we hear about people who are using herbs, organic food, and supplements to help with the treatment of illnesses. They are the oldest form of medicine used by healers worldwide and are commonly used by Indigenous people. Typically in Canada, they are used in conjunction with biomedicine, but some people use them on their own without any biomedicine (Royal College of Psychiatrists, 2016). You should consult a doctor before you use supplements or herbs because they can adversely affect some medication. Herbal remedies and supplements are plant-based vitamins and minerals (Royal College of Psychiatrists, 2016). Some of your clients may use herbal remedies because they do not have a healthcare plan that covers most of the cost of prescription medication. Approximately half of the mental health clients one of the authors (Rothwell) worked with stopped their drug therapy due to fear of addiction. As well, there are many religions in the world that do not endorse biomedical treatments such as blood transfusions.

TIME TO DEBRIEF

Colleen was placed in a home run by the province, which means that the province is responsible for her care. The staff support her growth and development and ensure her safety 24 hours a day, 7 days a week. As a staff member, Phoung thought it was important to know that she was making a difference in Colleen's life. For many human services professionals, that is why we enter this field in the first place—because we believe in making a difference. Sometimes clients take advantage of this. That is why it is important to maintain a professional boundary even though part of our role involves creating and facilitating relationships with our clients. When engaging in a worker/client relationship, we need to make sure that we have positive interactions that respect clearly defined boundaries. These boundaries need to be nonsexual and legitimate interactions that are of the helping nature (Dewane, 2010, p. 18). This issue is multifaceted and can become complicated. You need to make sure that you are careful with your clients because you can hurt them, cause more harm, or destroy your professional reputation by not establishing clear boundaries from the very beginning. You need to ensure that you do not blur the lines and that you follow your code of ethics (Dewane, 2010, p. 18). In order to maintain a professional relationship, you should not disclose to your client too much about your personal life. You must not have a sexual relationship, or even a friendship, with your client, either in person or online. Do not tell the client where you live (unless you are providing respite at your home), do not socialize with them outside of work, and do not attend their family functions as a personal friend.

Once you set up your boundaries and your client is aware of the type of relationship they can have with you—which is a working one—you will need to create connections in order for the client to feel safe so that they can ask for help, trust you, and be honest with you. Your role is to provide assistance, find resources, and help them to reach their goals in an ethical and healthy manner. We are in a helping profession because the clients need the help. It is not about us; it is about them. We need to consider what we are doing in case we are unknowingly making choices based on our needs and emotions rather than thinking objectively about how we can best meet the client's needs. Remember that policies and individualized service plans are created in the best interests of our clients, so follow these policies and plans to ensure that your client is receiving the best care possible. If you disagree with something, speak up and talk to management. The best thing we can do for our clients is to become their advocates, so advocate for change. It is a fact of life that not every client will like you, and to be honest, that is okay! Your job is not to be liked; it is to do your best to help your clients surpass their potential.

KEY CONCEPTS

Anxiety disorders
Attention deficit hyperactivity disorder (ADHD)
Communication book
Conduct disorders
Counselling
Depression
Eating disorders
Mood disorders
Naturopathy
Objective language
Observational skills
Poverty line
Psychotic disorders
Staff handbook
Substance abuse
Teratogens

IN THE PURSUIT OF KNOWLEDGE

1. Consult the Canada Food Guide. Did you know there is a version for First Nations, Inuit, and Métis people? How would you control Colleen's caloric intake and help her to maintain a healthy weight?
2. List some boundaries that you will establish with your clients when you are working in the field.
3. Explore the concept of a Johari Window.

4. Watch a clip of a *Mr. Bean* movie. What is his body language telling you? How can he communicate so much without saying a word?

5. What are the following actions communicating? Could any of the following be considered cultural?
   a. Tapping your foot
   b. Looking at the clock
   c. Smiling
   d. Crossing your arms over your chest
   e. Looking down
   f. Standing close

6. You are reading the communications book before starting your shift. Rewrite the following information provided by your colleague in order to respect confidentiality and make it more professional by changing the subjective language to objective language:

Today Colleen was whining about being hungry again. I followed her into the kitchen, knowing that she was going to get a snack. I said she could have one cookie. She said I was being mean to her. She said that Alex lets her have two cookies. I told her we had to follow the rules. Then she snapped. She had a wild look in her eyes. She grabbed a mug and hurled it at me, barely missing my head. I could have been killed. She was out of her mind. She was screaming and yelling mean things at me. She is a spoiled brat.

REFERENCES

Boyd, D., Johnson, P., & Bee, H. (2018). *Lifespan development* (6th Canadian ed.). Toronto: Pearson.

Canada Border Services Agency, Organized Crime Section. (2008, May). *Tattoos and their meanings*. Retrieved from https://info.publicintelligence.net/CBSA-TattooHandbook.pdf

Canadian Association of Naturopathic Doctors. (2016). Retrieved from www.cand.ca/index.php?49&L=0

Canadian Mental Health Association of British Columbia. (2014). *Mental illnesses in children and youth*. Retrieved from www.cmha.bc.ca/documents/mental-illnesses-in-children-and-youth-2/

Dewane, C. (2010). Respecting boundaries: The don'ts of dual relationships. *Social Work Today, 10*(1), 18.

Haas, M., & Mortensen, M. (2016, June). *The secrets of great teamwork*. Retrieved from https://hbr.org/2016/06/the-secrets-of-great-teamwork

National Institute of Mental Health. (2017a). *Attention Deficit Hyperactivity Disorder*. Retrieved from www.nimh.nih.gov/health/topics/attention-deficit-hyperactivity-disorder-adhd/index.shtml

National Institute of Mental Health. (2017b). *Psychosis*. Retrieved from www.nimh.nih.gov/health/topics/schizophrenia/raise/what-is-psychosis.shtml

Pimento, B., & Kernested, D. (2015). *Healthy foundations in early childhood settings* (5th ed.). Toronto: Nelson.

Preja, C. (2013). Verbal and non-verbal communication in sports culture. *Civilization and Sport, 14*(3), 239–243.

Royal College of Psychiatrists. (2016). C*omplementary and alternative medicines 1*. Retrieved from www.rcpsych.ac.uk/healthadvice/treatmentswellbeing/complementarytherapy.aspx

Schneider, S. (2009). The nature of symbols in the language of thought. *Mind and Language, 24*(5), 523–553.

Srebalus, D., & Brown, D. (2000). *A guide to the helping professions*. Boston: Allyn & Bacon.

Statistics Canada. (2015, July 8). *Low income lines, 2013–2014*. Retrieved from www.statcan.gc.ca/pub/75f0002m/75f0002m2015001-eng.pdf

Statistics Canada. (2017, May 26). CANSIM Table 206-0041—Low-income statistics by age, sex and economic family type, Canada, provinces and selected census metropolitan areas (CMAs). Retrieved from www5.statcan.gc.ca/cansim/a26?lang=eng&id=2060041

Wallace, J. (1972). The way I see it. *Canadian Medical Association Journal, 106*(7), 809.

Wood, J., & Schweitzer, A. (2009). *Everyday encounters: An introduction to interpersonal communication* (4th ed.). Scarborough, ON: Nelson.

SARA'S STORY

Hi! I'm Sara. I have been working for the provincial government as an early intervention specialist for the past few years. I work with preschools, daycares, day homes, and Head Start programs to help support early childhood educators, children, and their families.

Ted

Source: C. Genest

One day at work I was really discouraged. A new family started at one of our programs. The family had been in Canada for less than 72 hours and their two-year-old child, Ted, was placed in a child development centre. The family arrived with very little to their names. Ted wore the same two sets of clothes for months. By the time Ted arrived at the centre, his whole world had been turned upside down. He had just moved across the world, he did not speak English, and now his parents were leaving him with strangers for the first time in his life.

This day was very difficult for the early childhood educators. Ted spent the entire day crying, from the moment he was dropped off until the moment he was picked up. The director of the centre called me because she was heartbroken. Ted's entire life had changed in a very short time frame, and she was feeling helpless. He didn't understand what she was saying when she tried to calm him. He had no special blankets or comfort items because his family had come with so little. All the food was completely strange to him.

You have two options:

Option 1: Ted must be tired and overwhelmed. He should be at home with his
family. Turn to page 79.
Option 2: Be patient and keep getting to know Ted and his family. Turn to
page 83.

OPTION 1

Now, we know that Ted has experienced a lot of changes in his short life, and after
only 72 hours in a strange country, he has been placed in the care of people he does
not know. His parents are his foundation, his constant, his rock, and the only thing
that is familiar to him. Ideally, when a child starts at a centre, there is a transition
period to help them adjust to the new environment as well as to give the educators
a chance to get to know them. The first day, the child will come in for an hour with
a parent, the second day for part of the morning alone, and so on. Depending on
the child's age and temperament, the transition can be slower. Or they may be able
to start full days right afterwards. For Ted, the transition to a new country and an
unfamiliar centre in such a short period of time is disconcerting.

Before we get into the details, it is important to recognize that 21.9% of
Canadians were not born in Canada (Grenier, 2017). Canada is a relatively new
country whose foundation is based on immigration from other countries. Our
Indigenous population were the first peoples to live on the land, but immigration
to Canada is what created the country we live in today. The legislation for immigration, which began in 1869, was not always inclusive, which meant that people
from certain countries were barred from immigrating to Canada. Whereas today
Canadian immigration continues to be selective, it does not bar people based
on their nationality. Immigration policies do examine possible economic contributions, family reunification, and humanitarian reasons for seeking entry into
Canada (Bowal & Perry, 2013).

Humanitarian immigration most commonly refers to **refugees** who are
victims of persecution in their homeland. Simply stated, it is not safe for them
to return to their native land (Bowal & Perry, 2013). Recently, the Canadian
government admitted 25,000 Syrian refugees who were fleeing persecution and
war (Zimonjic, 2016). It is important to note that if someone has been convicted
of a serious crime, they cannot apply for asylum based on the fear of persecution.
Some individuals who have committed crimes cannot pass the security check and

will not be admitted to Canada. A person can apply for refugee status either after they have entered the country or while still outside. In this case, the Canadian government works with the United Nations High Commissioner for Refugees, other referral organizations, and private sponsors to facilitate resettlement in Canada (Bowal & Perry, 2013).

From reading Sara's story, we know that Ted recently immigrated to Canada. If he is a refugee, there is the possibility that he has experienced some trauma and that he is experiencing culture shock. Refugees are often displaced; some have been living in refugee camps, others have been separated from their families, some have lost their homes and communities, and many have little control over their situation. As human services professionals, we need to be aware of the challenges that immigrants and refugees face when they come to Canada. These challenges can include language barriers, cultural differences, educational attainment for children, obtaining employability skills, etc. Relocating to a new country or even a new community can be traumatic for anyone. Trauma is an experience that may affect a person's ability to cope. It has long-term effects that are both mental and physical. It is related to an event in a person's life that caused reactions, including an overwhelming feeling of helplessness and/or powerlessness. There are four main forms of trauma: simple, complex, developmental, and intergenerational (Poole & Greaves, 2012, p. 3). Trauma can have both psychological and physical symptoms that include but are not limited to a lack of emotional response; shame and fear; anxiety and panic attacks; problems with concentration; thoughts that get in the way of daily activities; flashback; problems sleeping, which lead to exhaustion (Centre for Addiction and Mental Health, 2012).

Trauma can affect children differently than adults. The brains of children exposed to chronic trauma and stress have been found to be different than those of children who have not experienced any trauma. When a person experiences stress or a threat, their brain's fight-or-flight response is activated through increased production of cortisol (Drexel University, 2013). Since children are constantly learning and developing, their childhood will set the foundation for the life they will have in the future. Jean Piaget (1932) created this theory based on his own observation of children. He believed that as a child grows, they change internally and their capacity to engage with the environment changes as well. Throughout a child's development, they experience states of disequilibrium and seek to return to a state of equilibrium. Thus, Option 1 (sending Ted home with his family) will be a gentle transition and assimilation into the new culture. The mechanisms Piaget proposed are two active processes: **assimilation** and **accommodation**.

Table 6: Assimilation and accommodation

Assimilation	The process of interpreting new information within the context of our existing cognitive structure.
Accommodation	When a child is accommodating new information based on the environment.

Source: Substance Abuse and Mental Health Services Administration, 2012

When both assimilation and accommodation are combined in a person, the tension between the two ongoing processes develop their cognitive abilities and capacities (Substance Abuse and Mental Health Services Administration, 2012).

Traumatic experiences that occur to children between birth and the age of six can have long-term consequences because children cannot always verbalize their reactions to the traumatic events. Their sense of safety may be shattered; they may experience fear, nightmares, and other negative reactions. Trauma can lead to behavioural and physiological symptoms, such as the ones Ted displayed in the daycare. Why does this happen? Children's developing brains are vulnerable, and trauma can affect a child's IQ, the regulation of their emotions, and the fears they may have (The National Child Traumatic Stress Network, 2010).

It comes as no surprise that trauma in childhood can have long-term effects. It is important for people who are considered at risk to find positive coping mechanisms in order to reduce the possibility of harm. There are coping strategies for youth who are experiencing trauma. By creating a sense of emotional and physical safety, levelling out power imbalances, and providing a safe and welcoming environment (The National Child Traumatic Stress Network, 2010), you will be able to help the child feel comfortable and learn. A few tips for helping a child who has experienced trauma are: use simple and positive language; make sure activities are developmentally appropriate so the child can experience success and thereby build up their confidence; observe changes in behaviour; create and adhere to a routine; and have boundaries but also show love (The National Child Traumatic Stress Network, 2010). Studies conducted in Canada have found that there is a high level of depression among young refugees and that most children and their families face disruptions to their educational and social development (Kirmayer et al., 2011, pp. 77–78).

The fact that Ted is coming to your centre means that he will be immersed in the English language. He needs to feel accepted and included in order to associate positive feelings towards his new cultural environment and the language spoken there. Teaching the other children at the centre some words in Ted's first language, like Sara did, will also help to enrich their environment and develop a sense of inclusion. As he is being immersed in English, Ted will experience the five stages of language acquisition.

Table 7: Five stages of language acquisition

Stage 1: Preproduction	Limited receptive vocabulary. They will repeat what you say. They will listen attentively.
Stage 2: Early production	They will begin to speak in short phrases that may not be grammatically correct.
Stage 3: Speech emergence	They can initiate short conversations. They will comprehend easy stories with illustrations.
Stage 4: Intermediate fluency	They are able to express more complex ideas and express their opinions. They will employ strategies from their first language to learn content in English.
Stage 5: Advanced fluency	Within five to ten years, their language acquisition is equivalent to that of a native speaker.

Source: Haynes, 2007, pp. 29–35

It is our role as professionals to support Ted's English language acquisition as well as to honour his first language so he will grow up to be bilingual or even multilingual. Researching the culture of our clients and learning some words in their native language is a positive and supportive way to help them be successful in their new country. Resources such as the federal government's travel website present the culture of most of the countries in the world. The website includes information on religion, food, the economy, the belief system, and the legal system. This can be a helpful resource when working with a population you are unfamiliar with. Canada is founded on multiculturalism, and we are proud to be such a diverse nation. For that reason, you will work with individuals of all faiths and customs over the course of your career. You may find that by doing a little research you are better able to serve your clients. By enriching your own knowledge you can create a welcoming environment and make their transition a more positive experience.

OPTION 2: SARA'S CHOICE

After a few days of seeing Ted being completely terrified and lost, I thought how easy it would be for us to learn a few words in his language. After talking with his mom, we came up with a list of everyday words. She went over the pronunciation with us. We now had some form of communication with Ted. We could communicate simple things like snack, nap, milk, banana, hello, goodbye, hug. It took about a month of us consistently using a mix of his language with English, paired with a warm, welcoming heart, for Ted to feel safe.

Most things slowly get better over time. In Ted's case, it was like a switch was flipped. He cried every day for just over a month. Then one day he went to sleep at nap time and woke up the happiest kid I have ever seen in my life. I had the joy of working with Ted and the educators for the next year. During that time he got upset only a handful of times. If he was upset and crying it was because he was hurt. He was a joyful, happy, outgoing boy, interacting with other children and participating in activities.

Ted's parents were so grateful for all we had done for the family. This was one of the first big challenges I had. It taught me to empower educators to change and adapt to the children's needs. Every child learns differently and has different needs and different stresses in their lives. We need to observe, act accordingly, and work together to find solutions.

The legislation for immigration, which began in 1869, was not always inclusive, which meant that citizens from certain countries were barred from immigrating to Canada. Whereas today Canadian immigration continues to be selective, it does not bar people based on their nationality. Immigration policies do consider possible economic contributions, family reunification, and humanitarian reasons for wanting to immigrate to Canada (Bowal & Perry, 2013).

Humanitarian immigration most commonly refers to refugees or refugee programs for individuals who are scared of persecution in their homeland. Simply stated, it is not safe for them to return to their native land (Bowal & Perry, 2013). Another category of immigration is the **independent immigrant** category, for immigrants with skills and experience who can enter the Canadian workplace. The **family reunification** category brings family members to Canada through the family sponsorship program. In order to sponsor a family member, an individual must be over the age of eighteen and be in good standing in Canada, with a minimum yearly income of $22,229. The purpose of these rules is to reunify families without affecting taxpayers. The most common type of sponsorship is by marriage. We have all heard stories of people from other countries marrying a Canadian in order to become a citizen. This is fraud; there are now programs in place to help minimize this occurrence (Bowal & Perry, 2013).

From reading Sara's story we know that Ted recently immigrated to Canada. If he is a refugee, there is the possibility that he has experienced trauma and/or **culture shock**. Refugees are often displaced; they live in refugee camps, they are often separated from their families, they lose their homes and communities, and they have no idea what the future holds for them. Once they arrive in Canada they often experience the following:

Table 8: Trauma and culture shock

Traumatic stress	The stress that occurs after harm that has affected their emotional and/or physical wellbeing.
Resettlement stressors	The stress they experience as they try to build a new home and start a new life.
Acculturation stressors	The stress that happens during integration into their new culture in comparison with their culture of origin.
Social isolation and discrimination	The stress of being a minority in a new country.

Source: Ellis, Murray, & Barrett, 2014

During the process of transitioning into a new culture, people often do not feel comfortable or have the ability to ask for help. As human services professionals, we need to be aware of the challenges that immigrants and refugees face when they come to Canada. They can include language barriers, cultural differences, educational attainment for children, job skills, etc. It is our role to research the culture of our clients so we can find a positive and supportive way to help create connections with them in order for them to make a successful transition to life in their new country. Resources such as the federal government's travel website present the cultural highlights for most countries in the world. The website includes information on religion, food, the economy, the belief system, and the laws. By doing a little research, you may find that you are better able to serve your clients and create a more welcoming environment.

In Ted's situation, it is obvious that his family has had some recent transitions. Human services providers should consider the **family-centred care model**, which recognizes that the family knows the child best, and as educators, we must respect the family's wishes, even if we do not agree with them. In Ted's case there are some definite cultural differences of which we may not be aware. Always remember your role is to become informed and learn how to work with the family. According to the Government of Alberta (2013), "the family has the primary responsibility for their children's well-being and development. When child care programs establish respectful, honest communication and joint decision-making with families, they enhance children's well-being and development. Families have a right to fully participate in their child's program" (p. 16). It is essential to take the time to get to know the families in your care. You can do this by having them fill out a questionnaire about the child's preferences and routines at home when they first come to register their child at your centre. Some centres even ask the family to come in for an interview and a tour before starting. You might want to hire an interpreter to facilitate this process. It is important that you analyze this information in order to ease the transition for the child by creating a link between what happens at home and what happens at the centre. Does the child nap in the morning and in the afternoon at home? This might become a problem if nap time only happens at the centre in the afternoon. The educator needs to work with the family to create a plan to move the child from two naps to one if they are ready to do so. Sara could have asked the mother for a recipe so they could prepare a familiar meal for Ted. (As Sara had noted, even the food was foreign to him.) It would be a good idea to involve the other children at the centre in the creation of the dish, even Ted's mother, and then encourage everyone to try it. All families could be invited to send in recipes, and you could create a cookbook for the centre or have a family night when each family brings in a dish to share.

Every province and territory has **licensing** regulations for child care centre that can sometimes make it impossible to respect the family's wishes if they are against the law or the licensing regulations. Some cultural practices may not be acceptable in the childcare setting. It is important to know the licensing regulations of your province/territory in order to ensure that you do not violate any regulations. If you have questions or concerns, you can always call the licensing officer and they can help you.

Ted's family is new to Canada, which can cause some language barriers depending on where the family is from. Do not automatically assume that people from other English-speaking or French-speaking countries will understand you. English in Ireland, for example, is different than Canadian English, and French from France is very different from the French spoken in New Brunswick. It is important that the questionnaire, registration forms, parent handbook, and newsletters be accessible for English-language learners. Depending on the languages spoken by your staff and the families, you may be able to print bilingual newsletters or have someone in your community explain the newsletters to the family. It is heartbreaking when a child cannot participate in an activity such as a field trip because the family did not understand that they had to sign the permission form. If you have limited resources in your community to help the family understand the newsletters, include images and visual references for the important words, and fill out the paperwork with the families in order to coach them through. There are computer programs and applications that you can purchase to help facilitate translation, but be wary of the quality of what they produce.

For all young children, including English-language learners, maintaining a fixed schedule and routine at a child care centre helps develop their vocabulary because it is repeated day after day. It is also reassuring to the children since they are able to predict what comes next, thereby reducing their anxiety and stress levels so they are able to learn. For example, after free play, we go to the bathroom, wash our hands, and sit down for snack. After snack, we go play outside. "Children thrive on having a consistent routine that provides a balance of activities designed to meet individual needs and foster physical, cognitive, social, and emotional growth. Best practices promote a daily schedule with large amounts of time for play, smooth transitions between activities, and a balance between child-initiated and teacher-directed activities" (Harms, Clifford, & Cryer, 2005, p. 5).

As the early intervention specialist, you want to work closely with the director of the centre to observe how the child and their family are adjusting. In the case of Ted's family, they may need to be referred to a counsellor to help them cope with the traumatic situation they have experienced, including the loss of loved ones. Look for and document any signs of culture shock, such as

1. anger, confusion, frustration;
2. isolation;
3. negativity towards their new country;
4. eating, drinking, or sleeping excessively; and
5. boredom, inability to concentrate. (Government of Canada, 2016)

A key to creating a helping relationship and ensuring the wellbeing of the children in your care is to check in with the family to see if their situation is improving, if they are receiving the supports they need and are beginning to transition. Hopefully, they have not been the victims of racism or discrimination in your community. Are they creating relationships with other families? Is their financial situation improving? Do they have safe and adequate housing? Depending on the size of your community, you might introduce the family to the intercultural centre or new-arrival centre, if you have one. Their transition can be made easier by becoming familiar with a local employment office, a food bank, and an agency that distributes donated clothing. Depending on the family's income and situation, the family may qualify for subsidized daycare, which means that a percentage of their childcare costs is covered by the provincial or territorial government.

TIME TO DEBRIEF

The **trauma-informed care model** is a model that we often use when working with refugees and immigrants. What exactly does this mean? It means that we maximize the individual's sense of safety. We do this because often clients have never truly felt safe, or they have lived the latest portion of their lives in fear. **Post-traumatic Stress Disorder (PTSD)** is always a concern (The National Child Traumatic Stress Network, n.d.). We work with the client to make new meaning of their trauma, their past, and their current experiences.

To be an effective helper you need to gain the ability to understand the needs of your clients. It is important to become informed about the culture and experiences of individuals on your caseload. This will help provide you with insight concerning your client, the situation they may be in, and any behaviours they may be exhibiting. Always remember that everyone has a story; it is your job as a human services professional to put the pieces together and arrive at a solution that meets the needs of everyone involved.

When in doubt, ask. If language is a barrier, many communities have programs where you can access a translator, and there is always the opportunity to use online translation programs. It is imperative that, regardless of our personal beliefs, we treat everyone with respect and dignity regardless of race, religion, sexual orientation, ability, or culture. Remember that each culture has its own cultural practices, and these may be important to the client's transition. If you have a foundational knowledge of these practices and are willing to help the clients by referring them to (or providing them with) the appropriate resources, you can help their recovery. In order to develop a healthy working relationship, you need to realize that you may not be able to provide all the services the client needs; therefore, you need to liaise with other agencies that can provide the services that will help your client to reach their goals for recovery and begin a new stage of their lives in Canada (Bolton et al., 2013, pp. 39–41).

KEY CONCEPTS

Accommodation
Acculturation stressors
Assimilation
Culture shock
Family-centred care model
Family reunification
Humanitarian immigration
Independent immigrant
Licensing
Post-traumatic Stress Disorder (PTSD)
Refugees
Resettlement stressors
Social isolation and discrimination
Trauma-informed care model

IN THE PURSUIT OF KNOWLEDGE

1. Find resources for English-language learners in your community.
2. Choose a country that you know nothing about. Tell your classmates about a holiday that country observes by explaining how they celebrate it.
3. Brainstorm some challenges new immigrants could face when they arrive in Canada. How could you help to ease their transition?

REFERENCES

Bolton, M., Buck, D., Conners, E., Kiernan, K., Matthews, C., McKellar, M., ... & Health Canada. (2013). *Trauma-informed: The trauma toolkit* (2nd ed.). Winnipeg: Klinic Community Health Centre. Retrieved from http://trauma-informed.ca/wp-content/uploads/2013/10/Trauma-informed_Toolkit.pdf

Bowal, P., & Perry, K. (2013). Categories for immigration to Canada. *Law Now, 38*(1). Retrieved from www.lawnow.org/categories-for-immigration-to-canada/

Centre for Addiction and Mental Health. (2012). *Trauma.* Retrieved from https://www.camh.ca/en/health-info/mental-illness-and-addiction-index/trauma

Drexel University. (2013). Center for Nonviolence and Social Justice, Dornsife School of Public Health. Retrieved from http://drexel.edu/cnvsj/

Ellis, H., Murray, K., & Barrett, C. (2014). Understanding the mental health of refugees: Trauma, stress, and the cultural context. In R. Parekh (Ed.), *The Massachusetts General Hospital textbook on diversity and cultural sensitivity in mental health* (pp. 165–187). New York: Humana Press.

Government of Alberta. (2013). *Alberta child care accreditation standards*. Retrieved from www.humanservices.alberta.ca/documents/accreditation-standards.pdf

Government of Canada. (2016). *Coping with culture shock*. Retrieved from https://travel.gc.ca/travelling/living-abroad/culture-shock

Grenier, E. (2017, October 25). 21.9% of Canadians are immigrants, the highest share in 85 years. *CBC News*. Retrieved from www.cbc.ca/news/politics/census-2016-immigration-1.4368970

Harms, T., Clifford, R. M., & Cryer, D. (2005). *Early childhood environment rating scale* (revised ed.). New York: Teacher's College Press. Retrieved from https://pdfs.semanticscholar.org/f321/8b9fa4ef40139d33745183b43e3ed2d50d18.pdf

Haynes, J. (2007). *Getting started with English-language learners*. Alexandria, VA: ASCD.

Kirmayer, L., Narasiah, L., Munoz, M., Rashid, M., Ryder, A., … & Pottie, K. (2011). Common mental health problems in immigrants and refugees: General approach in primary care. *Canadian Medical Association Journal, 183*(12), 959–967.

The National Child Traumatic Stress Network. (2010). *Early childhood trauma*. Retrieved from www.nctsn.org/trauma-types/early-childhood-trauma

The National Child Traumatic Stress Network. (n.d.). *Refugee trauma*. Retrieved from http://nctsn.org/trauma-types/refugee-trauma

Piaget, J. (1932). *The moral judgment of the child*. Glencoe, IL: The Free Press.

Poole, N., & Greaves, L. (Eds.). (2012). *Becoming trauma informed*. Toronto: Centre for Addiction and Mental Health.

Substance Abuse and Mental Health Service Administration. (2012). Retrieved from http://store.samhsa.gov/shin/content//ADM86-107/ADM86-1070R.pdf

Zimonjic, P. (2016, February 29). 25,000 Syrian refugees have landed, now for Phase 2, says John McCallum. *CBCNews/Politics*. Retrieved from www.cbc.ca/news/politics/refugee-mccallum-syria-canada-1.3469589

COWAN'S STORY

Hi! My name is Cowan. I have been working as a psychiatric aide for a long-term residential care facility for many moons. In my role, I provide assistance within the residential centre to my patients. I am responsible for following the treatment orders for the patients who have been assigned to me. Every shift, I am given a list of patients that I need to focus on and I take responsibility for their wellbeing. I help them complete their daily living activities (shower, brush teeth, prepare and eat meals) and I ensure that they are following their alternative treatments (such as art therapy) as dictated by their treatment order or as discussed by our unit nurse. I organize activities in the facility such as movie nights or an outing to the bowling alley, for example. Since I am a front line worker and the one who spends the most one-on-one time with my patients, it is also my responsibility to observe and report any unusual behaviour to the nursing staff and the unit managers.

Morgan

Source: C. Genest

My worst experience at work was the night I had a patient in a local psych ward in a public hospital. Sometimes, when our patients were extremely mentally or physically ill, we had to bring them to a local hospital that had additional services that our hospital couldn't provide. That night, I had to stay in a psych ward as a sitter. My patient was a twenty-year-old female who became quite violent and, because of this, had to have 24-hour supervision. If Morgan wasn't supervised, she would scream, kick, and lash out, unless she was in a wheelchair or a rocking chair—really anything that moved. We were in a psych ward where there weren't any rocking chairs, so I had to constantly push her in her wheelchair. When she was being pushed in the chair she would sit quietly. It was the only time she was calm. If you stopped pushing the wheelchair for any reason, she would become violent and self-harm.

That particular night, I thought I was set because there was a whole team of nurses and doctors and I thought they would help me. I didn't realize that I was very much on my own with my patient. When I started my shift, I thought I would be working with a team. The hospital's ward regulations stated that everyone had to be in their bedroom overnight while the ward was locked down. From nine o'clock at night to seven o'clock in the morning, patients had to stay in their rooms. The whole area is under camera and under lock and key. My shift had just started, so I started to push Morgan in her wheelchair down the hall, but at nine o'clock I was told I couldn't do that anymore and that she had to be locked down too. The rooms in the hospital are quite small and there wasn't any space for me to push Morgan back and forth in her room.

You have two options:

Option 1: Break the rules! Do what you think is best for the patient. If you choose this option, turn to page 93.
Option 2: Follow the rules and take her to her room. If you choose this option, turn to page 99.

OPTION 1

Under the Canada Health Act, health care in Canada falls under the responsibility of both the provincial/territorial and federal governments. The decisions concerning how the system is implemented and the budgetary implications are up to each provincial/territorial jurisdiction. The Act stipulates the primary characteristics of health care insurance and coverage within each province and territory (Minister of Justice, 2012). Specific health care funds have been made available to provide services for mental health and support the aging population. According to Goldner, Jenkins, and Bilsker (2016), there is a large and diverse amount of professional and nonprofessional services to address mental health concerns in the country (p. 285). Some examples of service providers include physicians, nurses, psychiatrists, social workers, early intervention workers, psychologists, occupational therapists, and child and youth care workers.

Each province and territory has its own **mental health act.**

Table 9: Mental health acts by province/territory

Alberta	Mental Health Act – Chapter M-13
British Columbia	Mental Health Act – Chapter 288
Manitoba	C.C.S.M.c M110 Mental Health Act
New Brunswick	Mental Health Act, R.S.N.B. 1973, c. M-10
Newfoundland and Labrador	Mental Health Care and Treatment Act
Nova Scotia	Bill No. 19, Mental Health Act
Northwest Territories	Mental Health Act – R.S.N.W.T. 1988, c. M-10
Nunavut	Mental Health Act (Nunavut) Section 76.05 of Nunavut Act, S.N.W.T. 1998, c. 34
Ontario	Mental Health Act, R.S.O. 1990, Chapter M. 7
Prince Edward Island	Mental Health Act – Chapter M-6.1
Quebec	Mental Patients Protection Act- Chapter P-41 Act Respecting the Protection of Persons Whose Mental State Presents a Danger to Themselves or to Others – Chapter P-38.001
Saskatchewan	Mental Health Services Act – Chapter M-13.1
Yukon	Mental Health Act – Chapter 150

The Mental Health Commission of Canada works collaboratively across the country within a framework to create a strategy for the recovery and wellbeing of Canadians. The Commission is a federally run agency which has proposed strategies that have been woven into health plans, annual objectives for psychiatric departments, community organizations, and hospital accreditation standards. The purpose of the strategy is to empower individuals with mental illness and their families to become active participants in their own care (Park et al., 2014, p. 1).

You may have heard of mental illness, mental health problems, mental distress, and mental disorders. These terms are based on the different degrees of severity that an individual may be experiencing. Symptoms of mental illness are described as positive or negative. Positive symptoms are abnormal thoughts, feelings, or behaviours that are not normally exhibited but are present in a person with mental illness, such as hallucinations. Negative symptoms are thoughts, feelings, or behaviours that are normally present but are decreased or absent in a person with mental illness. It is believed that "mental illness indirectly affects all Canadians at some time through a family member, friend or colleague. In any given year, 1 in 5 people in Canada will personally experience a mental health problem or illness. Mental illness affects people of all ages, educational, income levels, and cultures" (Canadian Mental Health Association, 2017, para. 1). Someone may experience short-term depression following the death of a loved one or after losing their job. This depression is not a mental illness, but rather a mental health problem. As discussed by McNally (2011), the boundaries between these definitions will never be clear because they depend on shifting political, cultural, and economic values. Because of this, we will never have clear-cut criteria for mental disorders (p. 212). As human services professionals, we need to be cautious of the terminology that we employ to avoid causing stigma. We need to be mindful of our choice of terminology because mental illnesses differ by kind and degree (McNally, 2011). For example, someone who has schizophrenia is very different from someone who is experiencing an anxiety disorder.

People interact and experience the world through their senses. This information is transmitted through the senses to the brain. "We constantly explore and examine new things—moving, smelling, tasting, feeling, looking, and listening—and thus discover their various properties. From this we can make decisions on whether or not we like the new object or experience" (Fowler, 2007, p. 15). "Some individuals are not able to organize and respond appropriately to these stimuli; others have lost skills due to accident or illness" and can become over- or understimulated when they are not able to control the amount of information surrounding them (Rompa, 2017). Sometimes classrooms have many different coloured bulletin boards on the wall or thematic items such as fall leaves hanging from the ceiling. This visual "clutter" can be overwhelming for some students with sensory processing disorder. Many schools and hospitals have created a room filled with resources and sensory material for people to explore. "**Snoezelen** multi-sensory environments are relaxing spaces that can help reduce agitation and anxiety, but they can also engage and delight the user, stimulate reactions and encourage communication" (Rompa, 2017). According to Rompa, the seven senses are as follows:

1. Vision (**visual**): Provides us with details about what we see and helps us to define boundaries as our brain processes colour, contrast, shape, and movement.
2. Touch (**tactile**): Keeps us in contact with our surroundings. Touch is vital to our survival and is one of our modes of communication. From head to toe, our skin helps us feel temperature, light touch, deep pressure, vibration, pain, and so much more.

3. Smell (**olfactory**): We use the sense of smell all the time. Flowery, pungent, musty, acrid, and putrid—we identify many things by their smells. Strong memories can also be tied to smells.
4. Hearing (**auditory**): Provides us with details about the sounds we hear, such as volume, pitch, rhythm, tone, and sequence.
5. Taste (**gustatory**): Gives us feedback on the different types of tastes—sweet or sour, spicy, salty, bitter, etc.
6. **Vestibular**: This sense puts balance in our lives. It provides information about movement, gravity, and changing head positions. It tells us whether we're moving or still, as well as the direction and speed of our movement. We may even tell whether we are vertically or horizontally positioned—even with our eyes closed.
7. **Proprioception**: This sense processes information from our muscles, joints, and other body parts to provide us with an unconscious awareness of the position of our body parts in relation to each other and their relation to other people and objects. (2017)

According to Dr. Lucy Jane Miller, there is also an eighth sense called interoception. "**Interoception** refers to sensations related to the physiological/physical condition of the body" such as hunger and thirst (STAR Institute for Sensory Processing Disorder, 2017). As a careful observer, Cowan would provide Morgan with sensory experiences in order to see how she would react. "The aim of providing sensory-focused activities is to activate or stimulate the sensory system. The effects of stimulating the sensory system can either be excitatory or inhibitory. Some kinds of sensory stimulation will make the person more alert and attentive, while others (e.g., massage) will have a relaxing effect" (Fowler, 2007, pp. 15–16). Cowan discovered that Morgan feels relaxed when she is rocking back and forth or riding in a wheelchair. Cowan then employs this knowledge and gives Morgan these opportunities to relax when she becomes agitated, thus providing positive behaviour support and increasing Morgan's ability to regulate her behaviour and emotions herself.

In addition to sensory-focused activities, there are many treatment options for mental illness, according to Goldner, Jenkins, and Bilsker (2016):

1. Psychopharmacotherapy is the use of medication for the treatment of psychiatric symptoms (p. 254).
2. Psychosurgery is brain surgery (p. 259).
3. Electroconvulsive therapy and magnetic seizure therapy induce seizures by passing an electric current through the brain (p. 257).

4. **Psychotherapy** includes cognitive behaviour therapy, play therapy, and motivational interviewing.
5. **Cognitive behaviour therapy** (CBT) focuses on identifying unrealistic thinking patterns and replacing them with positive or more beneficial ones (p. 262).
6. **Play therapy** allows children to express their thoughts and feelings through play (p. 263).
7. **Motivational interviewing** is a psychotherapy approach that focuses on helping clients use a non-judgmental method to consider their current situations and envision the changes they would like to see (p. 264).

Other treatment options are often used in collaboration with pharmaceutical treatments. **Complementary medicine** is a form of medicine that is used in conjunction with mainstream medical treatment (National Center for Complementary and Integrative Health, 2013). Complementary medicine is becoming more and more popular in the human services domain. Some of the most common forms of alternative medicine for individuals with mental illness are art therapy, nature therapy, and music therapy. Most psychiatric wards or hospitals include art therapy, animal-assisted therapy, or music therapy in addition to pharmacological treatment.

Art therapy provides the patient with the opportunity to draw, paint, or sculpt. The idea is that by creating art, the patient, as well as their human services professional, will become aware of their feelings. You can learn a lot about a person based on the story they tell through their creations. It can help individuals to have the opportunity to release their emotions and express them through art (Wong, 1998, p. 35).

In Paulette's story, we looked at genograms. You can make a genogram using art therapy techniques to understand the relationships and feelings a person experiences towards another member of their family. Art therapy is viewed not only as a method to improve psychological wellbeing but also as a way to promote the value of art in Canadian society and culture. Art as a therapeutic tool can work with all populations and ages and is an effective method of reaching individuals who are psychologically or physically ill.

Animal assisted therapy appears under the umbrella of **animal assisted interventions**. Animal assisted intervention involves working with animals in practice. Having a gerbil in a classroom or a dog in a therapeutic session are examples of this type of intervention. There are three main categories:

Table 10: Three categories of animal assisted interventions

Animal assisted activities (AAA)	Use of animals for education and recreation. Provide benefits to clients by enhancing their quality of life. E.g., a cat in a seniors' complex.
Animal assisted therapies (AAT)	Use of animals in interventions designed to help humans improve their overall wellbeing (social, physical, emotional, and cognitive). Animals are trained to deliver treatment to their handlers and others who need assistance. E.g., a dog that works with individuals with posttraumatic stress disorder.
Animal assisted education (AAE)	Use of animals for education. E.g., tadpoles to teach metamorphosis.

Source: Cirulli, Borgi, Berry, Francia, & Alleva, 2011

In animal assisted therapy, the animal provides the client with emotional support and comfort (Kruger & Serpell, 2006). Why would animal assisted therapy be beneficial for individuals like Morgan? In a therapy session, a dog, for instance, typically greets a client with enthusiasm. The dog seeks attention from the client and provides comfort, reducing the client's feelings of tension and stress. The animal can break the ice, providing a sense of security and trust (Giorgi, 2013). The animal helps the therapist create a positive connection, which then develops into a relationship from a shared point of interest. Often the animal helps the client feel unconditional love and becomes part of a non-judgemental atmosphere during the sessions (Giorgi, 2013).

Music therapy is another form of alternative therapy that is often used in the treatment of mental health. According to the Music Therapy Association of British Columbia (2016), music therapy is the skillful use of music to promote and restore physical, spiritual, mental, and emotional health. It is a process that includes creative, emotional, and structural therapeutic relationships to facilitate self-awareness and interaction with a therapist (MTABC, 2016). It is an evidenced-based clinical treatment that uses musical interventions to accomplish specific goals. For clients with a mental illness, music therapy can help build relationships. It can be used effectively with all age groups and has been known to modify the behaviour of children with developmental disorders and reduce agitation in patients with dementia (Canadian Association for Music Therapy, 2016).

Now that we understand a little more about what can be done to help regulate Morgan's behaviour, we need to address Cowan's behaviour. If she chooses to disobey the regulations and not return Morgan to her room during lockdown, Cowan could face the following repercussions: the nurse on duty could call security; Cowan could be reprimanded, removed from the hospital, or fired. Since Cowan is working for a different hospital that evening, there will be a unit manager on shift at her hospital who may be able to help by providing guidance and possibly a second employee to relieve her. If these options do not work, Cowan can always contact her union representative. Always remember that your personal safety is imperative. If you are not safe, it is your right to refuse to work alone. The hospital has to provide you with assistance because otherwise it could face legal consequences.

OPTION 2: COWAN'S CHOICE

> So I asked if I could take Morgan to the centre. It is attached to the hospital, so I could take her out of the unit and just walk with her all night, but they wouldn't let me. They said that Morgan had to be in her bedroom. I had to sit in her bedroom with her screaming and lashing out at me until seven o'clock the next morning. When I had to go to the bathroom I had to take Morgan with me. Because she wasn't moving, she started hitting me. They wouldn't help me at all. When my replacement arrived, I cried.

As human services providers, sometimes a challenging part of our jobs is to work with other members of the community. Morgan had a severe mental illness that required 24-hour, one-on-one care provided not only by the nursing staff but by a sitter. A **sitter** is someone who supervises and observes a patient. Sitters work in psychiatric hospitals or wards in nursing homes, where people may wander, or even in private homes. They make sure that the patient, visitors, and staff members are safe and observe the patient's behaviour to help identify any potential problems to others. As Cowan stated, because her patient was from a different hospital, it was her role to ensure that the patient and all those around her were safe. Sending a sitter from the hospital where Morgan usually resides could help her adjust to her new surroundings by providing a familiar worker and consistency in her routine. This would certainly support Morgan's transition behaviours by reducing the stress and anxiety that result from being in an unfamiliar place.

Since Cowan was working for a different hospital that night, she could contact the unit manager on shift at her regular hospital, who might be able to help by providing guidance and possibly a second employee to relieve her. Cowan always has the option to contact her union representative. Always remember that your personal safety is imperative. If you are not safe, it is your right to refuse to work alone. The hospital has to provide you with assistance because otherwise it could face legal consequences.

The Mental Health Commission of Canada works collaboratively across the country within a framework to create a strategy for the recovery and wellbeing of Canadians. The Commission is a federally run agency which has proposed strategies that have been woven into health plans, annual objectives for psychiatric departments, community organizations, and hospital accreditation standards. The purpose of the strategy is to empower individuals with mental illness and their families to become active participants in their own care (Park et al., 2014, p. 1).

It is pretty clear that Morgan's mental health treatment plan was based on the medical model for mental health. This is the primary form of treatment in Canada. The strategy for Yukon (2016) follows the framework for wellness that we discussed in Paulette's story. According to this framework, mental wellness is based on a balance that is enriched through education, caregiving activities, and cultural wellbeing (p. iv). Yukon Territory (2016) follows eight principles:

1. Person-centred
2. Culturally responsive
3. Integrated and coordinated
4. Builds capacity
5. Full continuum
6. Evidence-based practice and design
7. Accountable and ongoing evaluation
8. Across a lifespan

Person-centred care is an evidence-based approach to working with clients to ensure that their treatment needs are met. The client has a say in the planning, implementation, and monitoring of their needs. The program is customized for each client (Talerico, O'Brien, & Swafford, 2003, p. 13). According to the document *Forward Together: Yukon Mental Wellness Strategy* (Yukon Health and Social Services, 2016), cultural responsiveness means ensuring that the services provided are diverse and inclusive (p. 21). Integration and coordination means an individual can enter at any point into the mental health system and the system will coordinate the services required based on the individual's needs (p. 21). Building capacity focuses on the development and the ability of front line service providers to ensure access and support in the community in order to match an appropriate service with the client in need (p. 21). Full continuum includes all spectrums of the human services field—promotion, community development and education, prevention, early intervention, assessment, treatment, trauma informed, long-term treatment, palliative care, and research (p. 22).

Throughout your academic experience, you will hear about **evidence-based practice**. Evidence-based practice bridges the gap between what is known and what is done in practice. This means that professionals are conducting treatment based on research because the evidence shows that it works (McCabe, 2006, p. 50). Accountability is imperative when we are working with vulnerable people because the outcomes can affect our clients for the rest of their lives. As discussed in *Forward Together: Yukon Mental Wellness Strategy*, ongoing evaluations of the strategy will help evolve best practices (Yukon Health and Social Services, 2016, p. 22). Once a program has been created and implemented, it needs to be evaluated to ensure that it is going well and that everything is working. Through evaluation, the services providers can ensure that their clients' needs are being met. Human services and programs often focus on providing service to specific age groups, such as Early Learning and Child Care, which focuses on young children and their families; Child and Youth Care, which focuses on children and adolescents at risk; Social Work, Child and Family Services; adult services and programs; and senior services 55+, which cover the entire lifespan.

Cowan was concerned that Morgan was harming herself. Intentional **self-harm** includes "purposely self-inflicting poisoning or injury" (Canadian Institute for Health Information, 2014). There are many different reasons why a person may self-harm—for a release of tension and internal pain, for an adrenaline rush, because of an addiction, or in order to feel included. For individuals with developmental disabilities or a mental illness, self-harm is a method of coping when they become overstimulated. Self-injury is not necessarily an attempt to end one's life. Many youth and children self-harm because it gives them control of their situation or their body. A victim of sexual abuse may cut her stomach to try to regain control of her body. If she cuts her stomach, her perpetrator will no longer know what it looks like. It is important that this form of communication be recognized and that the person receives help before they lose their life.

One of the concerns when working with individuals who have a mental illness, or who experience loss or trauma, is suicide. We often put patients such as Morgan on suicide watch when they demonstrate behaviours such as self-harm or verbalize that they want to die, or if they have attempted suicide in the past. When working with a client who has stated that they wish to end their life or the lives of others, it is imperative that you call 911 and help the client create a safety plan until help arrives. Verbalizing the desire to end one's life is not attention-seeking behaviour. In hospitals and prisons, the patient on suicide watch is put in a safe room without any objects, is constantly monitored either on a television screen or in five- or ten-minute checks, and is given psychological assistance. Once they are deemed to be no longer a threat to themselves or to others, they are released from the suicide watch.

TIME TO DEBRIEF

Cowan chose to follow the rules even though her personal safety was at risk. By choosing to obey the regulation and return to her client's room during lockdown, she put both herself and Morgan at risk for harm, which is against our ethics and values. An unspoken rule in human services is that everyone should be safe from harm or abuse. It is unethical to place an employee and/or a client in a situation in which they could be harmed.

Cowan needed to act beforehand to advocate for continuity of care. The problem is that she didn't know who to approach. In order to find out the name of the patient advocate for that hospital, she would start by asking the unit manager. If that did not work, she would need to address the person at the next level of the hierarchy. Some hospitals, like those in Saskatchewan, refer to the people in this role as quality of care coordinators; others refer to them as patient advocates. In some cases, you may need to call your provincial or territorial **ombudsman**, whose role it is to help with complaints of unfair treatment by a provincial or territorial government authority or program. You can also contact the human rights commission for assistance. If you are not sure who to contact, just ask. Remember that this is for the wellbeing of a vulnerable person who needs your help to have their voice heard. Present your case in a professional, respectful, and objective manner and provide viable alternatives you believe would be possible ways to resolve the situation. Always remember to stay safe, because your safety is important for your wellbeing and that of your family, and in the end, that of your clients.

When considering Cowan's situation we need to be aware of the risk of **counter-transference**, which is defined as "the redirection of childhood emotions felt by an analyst towards a patient" (Barber, 2005); when the unconscious needs of a counsellor, therapist, or human services professional conflict with their understanding of the client's experiences (Reich, 1951, p. 154). It is important for human services professionals to be aware of their boundaries in order to reduce the likelihood of counter-transference. Because we work with vulnerable people daily, we may develop strong feelings based on our client's past and their previous relationships. Hearing the stories of clients who have experienced violence and persecution will directly impact you. You may feel overwhelmed by the emotions expressed by your clients when you learn about their stories and their situations. In some cases it is very difficult to remain neutral, but it is your role as a professional to be empathetic and present without taking on the client's pain or emotional response. It is important to recognize that in some cases you may be the only person with whom your client feels they can have a meaningful conversation (Alayarian, 2004, p. 43). If you get emotionally involved, the situation becomes dangerous. When you become emotionally involved, you can no longer have perspective on the situation. It will be difficult to conduct interventions in an ethical manner and find assistance because you have put yourself in a vulnerable position.

KEY CONCEPTS

Animal assisted interventions
Animal assisted therapy
Art therapy
Auditory
Cognitive behaviour therapy
Complementary medicine
Counter-transference
Evidence-based practice
Gustatory
Interoception
Mental health act
Motivational interviewing
Music therapy
Olfactory
Ombudsman

Person-centred care
Play therapy
Proprioception
Psychotherapy
Self-harm
Sitter
Snoezelen
Tactile
Vestibular
Visual

IN THE PURSUIT OF KNOWLEDGE

1. Find one organization or program in your community that provides services for individuals with mental illness. Provide information about the program, list what services it provides, determine the benefits, and state why the program is important for the people in your community.
2. There are many forms of alternative medicines. Choose two that were not mentioned in this chapter and describe them in detail.
3. What would you put in a Snoezelen room?
4. Role play what you would say to your unit manager to advocate for Morgan in this situation.

REFERENCES

Alayarian, A. (2004). Counter-transference in working with refugees. *Self & Society, 32*(5), 42–45.

Barber, K. (Ed.). (2005). *Oxford Canadian dictionary* (2nd ed.). New York: Oxford University Press. http://dx.doi.org/10.1093/acref/9780195418163.001.0001

Canadian Association for Music Therapy. (2016). *What is music therapy?* Retrieved from www.musictherapy.ca/about-camt-music-therapy/about-music-therapy/

Canadian Institute for Health Information. (2014). *Intentional self-harm among youth in Canada*. Retrieved from www.cihi.ca/web/resource/en/info_child_harm_en.pdf

Canadian Mental Health Association. (2017). *Fast facts about mental illness*. Retrieved from https://cmha.ca/media/fast-facts-about-mental-illness/

Cirulli, F., Borgi, M., Berry, A., Francia, N., & Alleva, E. (2011). Animal-assisted interventions as innovative tools for mental health. *Annali dell'Istituto Superiore Di Sanita, 47*(4), 341–348.

Fowler, S. (2007). *Sensory stimulation*. London: Jessica Kingsley Publishers.

Giorgi, Z. (2013). Pet therapy: Animal-assisted activities/therapy 101. *Pet Partners*. Retrieved from https://petpartners.org/

Goldner, E., Jenkins, E., & Bilsker, D. (2016). *A concise introduction to mental health in Canada* (2nd ed.). Toronto: Canadian Scholars' Press.

Kruger, K., & Serpell, J. (2006). Animal-assisted interventions in mental health: Definitions and theoretical foundations. In A. H. Fine (Ed.), *Handbook on animal-assisted therapy* (2nd ed.). New York: Elsevier.

McCabe, L. (2006). Evidence-based practice in mental health: Accessing, appraising, and adopting research data. *International Journal of Mental Health, 35*(2), 50–69.

McNally, R. (2011). *What is mental illness?* Cambridge, MA: The Belknap Press of Harvard University Press.

Minister of Justice. (2012). Consolidation: Canada Health Act—Chapter C-6. Retrieved from http://laws-lois.justice.gc.ca/PDF/C-6.pdf

Music Therapy Association of British Columbia. (2016). *What is a musical therapist?* Retrieved from www.mtabc.com/what-is-music-therapy/what-is-a-music-therapist/

National Center for Complementary and Integrative Health. (2013). *Complementary, alternative, or integrative health: What's in a name?* Retrieved from https://nccih.nih.gov/health/integrative-health

Park, M., Zafran, H., Stewart, J., Salsberg, J., Ells, C., Rouleau, S., ... & Valente, T. (2014). Transforming mental health services: A participatory mixed-methods study to promote and evaluate the implementation of recovery-oriented services. *Implementation Science, 9*(1), 119.

Reich, A. (1951). On counter-transference. In R. Langs (Ed.), *Classics in psychoanalytic technique* (pp. 153–160). Oxford: Rowman & Littlefield Publishers Inc.

Rompa. (2017). *Snoezelen multi-sensory environments*. Retrieved from www.snoezelen.info/

STAR Institute for Sensory Processing Disorder. (2017). *Your 8 senses*. Retrieved from www.spdstar.org/basic/your-8-senses

Talerico, K., O'Brien, J., & Swafford, K. (2003). Aging matters. Person-centered care: An important approach for 21st century health care. *Journal of Psychosocial Nursing & Mental Health Services, 41*(11), 12–16.

Wong, C. (1998). What is this "art therapy"? *Canadian Art Therapy Association Journal, 12*(1), 34–40.

Yukon Health and Social Services. (2016). *Forward together: Yukon mental health wellness strategy 2016–2020*. Retrieved from www.hss.gov.yk.ca/pdf/mentalwellnessstrategy.pdf

JEAN-STÉPHANE'S STORY

B onjour! My name is Jean-Stéphane. I work for a non-profit organization of-fering family intervention services. I have been a family support coordinator for two years. A family support coordinator is a human services professional who helps vulnerable families. I coordinate supports for individuals and families by helping with housing and rehabilitative services; I coordinate access to services for families that are experiencing trauma; and I often work with child and family services in a supervisory role during family visitations.

The baby

Source: C. Genest

We were working through a family group conference. The mother and father had all kinds of things going on between them. They hated each other's guts, first of all, and were very manipulative with their own families, trying to make them believe all kinds of lies and awful things about each other. Both families hated the mother and father. Everybody hated everybody else. It was very much one side versus the other. The mother and father had drug issues. The mother had a new boyfriend who had a very violent past. She was quite happy with him because she felt that he was going to protect her from whatever she was getting herself into with drugs. It was very messed up. It was an interesting way of thinking. This was not a safe place for a child. At this point, social services told the parents their baby could not stay with either one of them. The mother and father were not stable, but their aim was to have the baby stay within the family, a blood relation. None of the relatives lived in the area near them.

❧

You have two options:

Option 1: Let's try to keep the baby in the family. If you choose this option, turn to page **109**.
Option 2: Suggest that the baby be placed under the care of the province/territory. If you choose this option, turn to page **113**.

OPTION 1: JEAN-STÉPHANE'S CHOICE

Setting up this family group conference was a very interesting challenge. We could not all meet at the office. I was wondering how we were going to do this. We figured out finally that we were going to Skype several people and phone conference several others. The only people in the room were the mother, the father and me, with a social worker who came in and out but didn't stay. So it was just the three of us, with four people on the phone and three on Skype—seven very angry people talking through speakers. The conversation went back and forth, back and forth. I was there as a facilitator so I was not involved in the conversation.

Eventually, my role turned very much into mediator when I had to step in and set boundaries—for example, no name calling. The mother and father were in agreement with the plan to look after the baby. There was one person from each side of the family, two people in total, who were willing to take the baby, very nice, very stable people. But when we'd get to the point when the mother and father would come to a decision, the social worker would come back into the room and the mother and father would start fighting and back out of the plan. This happened three or four times. I would call the social worker from her office, she would come to our office and ask, "What's the plan?" I'd say, "This is what we've laid out, this is the deal. Mrs. X is going to take the baby." Then a member of one family would say no and the other family would blow up. This happened about four times over six hours. By this time, everybody was exhausted, everybody was angry. Then the two groups of speakers got into a huge yelling match and the mother and father became even more stressed.

Finally, I made the call and said that it was their last chance, if they couldn't be civil—because it was turning into name calling and calling people out on things they'd done in the past, not a good situation whatsoever—if you couldn't talk rationally, I was going to hang up. End of story. So I hung up the phone and hung up the Skype. The mother, the father, and I sat there and I asked, "So what are we doing?" It took only half an hour for them to come up with a solution. They both signed off on it, it was done.

I think the lesson I got out of this case is that sometimes the family can be very helpful, but sometimes the client needs to recognize when the family is not being helpful. Especially when they get defensive about their own family. But the fighting was harming the baby. It wasn't in the baby's best interest.

We ended up finding a good home for the baby that was within the family, just not the family members who were talking that day. Surprisingly, I actually got a text saying that Ms. W. was now willing and able to take the baby.

Every family's circumstances vary, but most families that are part of the Canadian child welfare system ended up there because someone suspected child abuse or neglect and contacted the agency. **Child welfare** is a term that is used to describe a set of private as well as government services designed to protect a child from abuse and provide the family with supports. Child welfare agencies will investigate allegations, supervise foster care, and in some cases arrange adoptions. They also provide supports to help a family stay together as a unit. In Canada, all provinces and territories have agencies that can be contacted 24 hours a day to help ensure the safety of all children in our nation. While every agency is different, there is a standard protocol they must all follow:

1. The agency receives a complaint of possible abuse.
2. They investigate the claim.
3. They provide services to the family and the child, such as:

    *   Arrange for the child to live with family members.
    *   Arrange for the child to live with a foster family.
    *   Place the child in foster care.
    *   Place the child in a group home.
    *   Implement the family enhancement act.
    *   Arrange permanent adoptive homes.
    *   Arrange for independent living services for youth in foster care. (Wegner-Lohin & Boatswain-Kyte, 2014)

The way child welfare programs are implemented and the process of **protection services** are different for each province and territory. Child welfare is a decentralized system, which means that it falls under provincial and territorial jurisdiction. Each province or territory has its own government agency responsible for child welfare and its own legislation. It is the role of the human services professional to be aware of the legislation and the governing agency in their province or territory. It is also important to note that First Nations, Métis, and urban Aboriginal child and family service agencies also exist, and they can be affected by federal legislation as well as provincial or territorial legislation (Wegner-Lohin & Boatswain-Kyte, 2014).

Guardianship orders fall under numerous different terminologies and age categories in each provincial and territorial jurisdiction (see Table 11).

Jean-Stéphane had already decided that the baby needed to be removed from the biological parents' care, but he wanted to keep the baby in the family. Since two people were willing to look after the child, protective services needed to become involved. This process involves completing a family assessment through an investigation and according to Section 1(2) of the Child, Youth and Family Enhancement Act:

> A child is considered to be in need of intervention when there are reasonable grounds to believe that their survival, the development of the child or their security is endangered to one or more of the following:
>
> 1. Guardian of the child is dead.
> 2. They have been abandoned or lost.
> 3. Neglect (inability to provide basic needs or adequate supervision).
> 4. The child has been or is at risk of abuse (sexual, physical, emotional).
> 5. The child has been subjected to cruel punishment.
> 6. The guardian of the child is unable to protect them from abuse or maltreatment. (Alberta Queen's Printer, 2000, c, C-12)

The first step is an **apprehension order**, which allows the agency to take the child from their custodial guardian (the baby's parents). In some situations the court makes a **supervision order** stating that the child be returned to their guardian but an agency such as Child and Family Services needs to conduct regular visitations to ensure that the child's needs are being met. This period usually lasts for less than six months. The court may order the parents to take treatment for addictions, parenting classes, etc. In Jean-Stéphane's case, he could

Table 11: Guardianship orders by province/territory

Province/Territory	Legislation	Age
Alberta	Child, Youth and Family Enhancement Act Drug-endangered Child Act Protection of Sexually Exploited Children Act	< 18
British Columbia	Child, Family and Community Services Act Adoption Act	< 19
Manitoba	Child and Family Services Act (1985) Child and Family Services Authorities Act (2003)	< 18
New Brunswick	Family Services Act Intercountry Adoption Act	< 16
Newfoundland and Labrador	Child, Youth and Family Services Act Children and Youth Care and Protection Act Adoption Act	< 16
Northwest Territories	Child and Family Services Act	< 16
Nova Scotia	Children and Family Services Act Children and Family Services Regulations Adoption Information Act	< 16
Nunavut	Child and Family Services Act	< 16
Ontario	Child and Family Services Act Children's Law Reform Act Family Law Act	< 16
Prince Edward Island	Child Protection Act Adoption Act	< 18
Québec	Youth Protection Act	< 18
Saskatchewan	Adoption Act Child and Family Services Act Emergency Protection for Victims of Child Sexual Abuse and Exploitation Act	< 16
Yukon	Children's Act Child and Family Services Act Child and Youth Advocate Act	< 19

* Please note that children who are considered to be vulnerable (those who have a mental or physical disability) may be eligible for services until the age of 19. This is based on provincial/territorial assessment criteria.

recommend that both parents seek treatment. In order to choose treatment, you need to assess both parents. Do they have health care plans to cover the cost? You need to find addiction programs such as a detoxification program. Typically, this program lasts seven days, then the client is put on a wait list for rehabilitation. This is dependent upon funding.

Free programs are funded by the province/territory. Every province/territory has a certain number of beds allocated for free treatment. It is your role to research the facilities and place your client on a wait list. While they are waiting for a spot, contact addictions services in your region and set the client up with an addictions counsellor. Most communities have an Alcoholics Anonymous (AA) program and/or a Narcotics Anonymous (NA) program. Something to consider when doing this referral is the client's religion. AA and NA are Christian based. If your client is not a Christian, inform them about this aspect of AA and NA and let them decide if they want to join. The client should contact their family doctor. If they are abusing drugs and alcohol, they may have done some damage to their bodies. The doctor may be able to refer them to a hospital-based program.

A **temporary guardianship order** or **TGO** is a court order granting temporary custody of a child to an adult with the hope that the child's parents will eventually be able to regain custody if they are able to meet the requirements set out by the courts. A **permanent guardianship order** or **PGO** is when the court finds that the survival and wellbeing of the child is in jeopardy with their current guardian; therefore it is unlikely that the guardian will regain custody, and permanent custody will be granted to another adult who will care for the child.

OPTION 2

Child welfare describes a set of private and government services designed to protect a child from abuse and provide the family with supports. Child welfare agencies will investigate allegations, supervise foster care, and in some cases arrange adoptions. They can also provide supports to help a family stay together as a unit. In Canada, all provinces and territories have agencies that can be contacted 24 hours a day to help ensure the safety of all children in our nation. Every family's circumstances will vary, but most families that are a part of the Canadian child welfare system are there because someone suspected child abuse or neglect and contacted the agency.

In 2011, there were 47,885 children living in foster care in Canada (Kirkey, 2012). Canada favours a **signs of safety (SOS)** approach, meaning that the child needs to be considered at risk to be removed from their home. "The SOS model guides work in partnership with families and children to increase safety and reduce risk and danger by focusing on strengths, resources, and networks the family have" (Government of Alberta, 2016). Once a decision has been made to remove a child from the home, they may be placed in foster care.

A child in foster care is referred to as a child in care (Farris-Manning & Zandstra, 2003, p. 1). All provinces and territories in Canada have legislative responsibility for children placed under the care of child and family services. One exception is the federal responsibility for First Nations People with status. Each province and territory has legislation that defines how a child will be protected from abuse and neglect. Each jurisdiction has its own policies and structure (Farris-Manning & Zandstra, 2003, p. 1). Nationally, family-based care is the preferred option, meaning that the child is placed with a family member. It is a cost-effective method that allows the child to stay connected with their family.

> Kinship care is a family home that is approved to care for a child in need because of a family connection or significant relationship to the child (e.g., grandparent, aunt, close family friend). Kinship caregivers provide:
>
> - a child with love and care in a familiar setting
> - parents with a sense of hope that their child will remain connected to their birth family
> - families with a sense of trust, stability, and comfort
> - an ability to support and maintain lifelong traditions and memories
> - support to a child in building healthy relationships within the family
> - guidance and reinforcement of a child's cultural identity and positive self-esteem. (Government of Alberta, 2017)

Once the baby was apprehended, what would be the next steps? The child would become a permanent **ward of the Crown** and would fall under a permanent guardianship order. When a child is a ward of the Crown, their provincial/ territorial government is responsible for their care until they become of legal age. Children are often placed in group homes or foster care. It is the responsibility of the Crown to make all decisions concerning the child's wellbeing, including medical care. It should be noted that in many provinces, when a child becomes a ward of the Crown, a plan for the child's care must be presented outlining the arrangements made to address the child's wellbeing.

TIME TO DEBRIEF

Regardless of the option you chose, you need to follow the **law**. The law is a consistent set of universal rules that have been published, are widely known, and are accessible. They are generally accepted by society and enforced by local judicial workers and police officers. These rules describe the way people are required to act in society and the expectations that a society has for its members. In Canada, the law is established by the federal and provincial government and based on our values as a nation and a society (Canadian Superior Courts Judges Association, 2016). We have two main streams of law: **civil law** and **public law** (see Table 12).

Since the custody of the child is in question, the case will be heard in a court of civil law, where it will be determined what will be in the best interest of the child. Jean-Stéphane decided to go down the path of keeping the child with family members because he believes in **kinship care**. Historically, the family unit has been responsible for its children by providing protection, care, and the basic necessities of life. When children were not able to be cared for by their parents, their parents found them a home with their extended family (Denby, 2016, p. 42). There has been a need to find permanent homes for children who are in, or could be in, the child welfare system. "The preference for placing children with kin is a prominent practice strategy used today" (Denby, 2016, p. 43). Placing children in kinship care provides them with a sense of permanency that will hopefully facilitate stability and contribute to their overall wellbeing. According to evolutionary psychology, which was influenced by Darwin (1958), theorists believed that parental investment flows from the parents' interest in the survival

Table 12: Law in Canada

Civil law	Public law
Relationships between individuals, including family law	Matters that affect society and the collective sense of security. Includes criminal law and administrative law
Contracts, property ownership, rights and obligations of family members, damage to property, damage to property caused by others, wrongful dismissal of employees	Criminal law: crimes or acts of harm (intentional) against an individual and/or offences against society. Considered an offence against society because it violates a collective sense of security.
Family law: divorce, parental responsibility, custody agreements	

Source: **Department of Justice Canada, 2005**

of their children. Individuals can also be heavily invested in the survival of their kin (Denby, 2016, p. 144). One problem that can be seen in Jean-Stéphane's story is that everyone involved may have been reluctant to enter into an adoptive relationship because it could cause family problems. Instead of adopting, some families favour guardianship care, in which the foster parents gain guardianship status, becoming the child's permanent care provider (Farris-Manning & Zandstra, 2003, p. 2).

KEY CONCEPTS

Apprehension order

Child welfare

Civil law

Kinship care

Law

Permanent guardianship order (PGO)

Protection services

Public law

Signs of safety (SOS)

Supervision order

Temporary guardianship order (TGO)

Ward of the Crown

IN THE PURSUIT OF KNOWLEDGE

1. Considering this case, was the baby exposed to a teratogen? What are some of the signs and symptoms you would look for?
2. Have you ever worried about the wellbeing of a child? If so, what did you do?
3. What do you believe should happen to children who do not have families to care for them?
4. Time to debate. One side supports the foster care system, one side is against it.
5. Research the supports that are in place in your community to assist foster children who "age out" of the system.
6. Please fill out the family case plan form found in the appendix, using Jean-Stéphane's case.

REFERENCES

Alberta Queen's Printer. (2000). *Child, Youth and Family Enhancement Act.* Retrieved from www. qp.alberta.ca/documents/Acts/c12.pdf

Canadian Superior Courts Judges Association. (2016). *The rule of law.* Retrieved from www. cscja-acjcs.ca/rule_of_law-en.asp?l=4

Denby, W. (2016). *Kinship care: Increasing child well-being through practice, policy, and research.* New York: Spring Publishing Company.

Department of Justice Canada. (2005). *Canada's system of justice.* Retrieved from www.justice. gc.ca/eng/csj-sjc/just/img/courten.pdf

Farris-Manning, C., & Zandstra, M. (2003). *Children in care in Canada.* Child Welfare League of Canada. Retrieved from http://cwrp.ca/sites/default/files/publications/en/ ChildrenInCareMar2003Final.pdf

Government of Alberta. (2016). *Government of Alberta and Western Australia implement largest international system-wide implementation of Signs of Safety: Key facts.* Retrieved from: www. humanservices.alberta.ca/documents/signs-of-safety-factsheet.pdf

Government of Alberta. (2017). *Kinship care.* Retrieved from www.humanservices.alberta.ca/ foster-kinship-care/14907.html

Kirkey, S. (2012, September 19). Census 2011: Canada's foster children counted for first time. *National Post.* Retrieved from http://nationalpost.com/news/canada/ census-2011-canadas-foster-children-counted-for-first-time

Wegner-Lohin, J., & Boatswain-Kyte, A. (2014). Alberta's child welfare system. *Canadian Child Welfare Research Portal.* Retrieved from http://cwrp.ca/sites/default/files/publications/en/AB_ infosheet_final.pdf

RENÉE'S STORY

My name is Renée. I work as a supervisor in a daycare. We are licensed to care for up to twenty-four children ages twelve months up to six years who have not yet started Grade 1. I have three full-time staff members and two casual staff members, including the cook. I was recently asked what my best day on the job was. Honestly, I have to tell you that's a tough question. Here is the situation …

Little boy
Source: C. Genest

Okay, there was not a great relationship between mother and father; they were separated. It was a split-up family, with a little guy who was attending my daycare. My centre was trying to support the family in order to support the little boy. The father had a history of drugs, abuse, and problems with the law. The mother obviously had trust issues and did not want the father to be involved in the child's life. The son had a bond with his father and obviously missed him a great deal, which led to aggressive behaviours such as biting and hitting. The father was in a new relationship, but the mother did not get along with the new girlfriend. I knew the little boy missed his dad because he drew pictures of him, talked about him constantly, and every intervention ended with a conversation about dad. Now how could a good day come out of this situation?

You have two options:

Option 1: Stay out of it. It's not your job to deal with dad. If you choose this option, turn to page **121**.
Option 2: What a pickle! How can you help this family? If you choose this option, turn to page **126**.

OPTION 1

By choosing this option, you will stay out of the family's personal problems; however, there are a number of things that you can do in order to support the mother and her son, who continue to be your clients. The first thing is to establish parental rights. You need to ask if there is a **court order**. A court order includes instructions outlining how an individual is going to interact with the child. According to the court order, who has been awarded custody of the child? The court could have assigned joint custody or sole custody, with or without visitation rights. Always follow the instructions provided by the judicial system.

Is there a **restraining order** that forbids the father from making contact with, or being in the vicinity of, the mother and/or the child? The term "restraining order" may be different in other provinces and territories. In British Columbia, for example, a restraining order is referred to as a protection order. It is established by a police officer or a judge to help protect one individual from another. A restraining order means that there is to be no contact, or only limited contact, between two people, or that there are certain conditions that must be followed—for example, the parent is allowed supervised visits and cannot be alone with the child (Government of British Columbia, 2017). You will need to see this document and its conditions before you can release the child into the father's care. If you feel that the father has violated the restraining order, contact the police and/or social services immediately.

There are two types of protection orders in British Columbia. The first type is a **peace bond**, which is established by the criminal code of Canada. A peace bond protects a person from anyone, including a former partner. You do not need a lawyer to get a peace bond, but you need to call the police department to ask for one. If the application for the peace bond proceeds, the crown counsel becomes involved, which means that if the case it goes to court it will go to criminal court (Government of British Columbia, 2017).

The second type of protection order is a **family law protection order**, which is made under the Family Law Act. It protects a person from a family member, including a former or current partner, a parent, or a guardian. A family law protection order does not involve the criminal justice system and it can be applied for under family law (Government of British Columbia, 2017). It is important for all parties involved in the protection order to follow the guidelines set out for them. If the conditions are not met, the police can issue a warrant for the arrest of the person who is in violation of the conditions. They could be charged with an offence for breaching the order (Government of British Columbia, 2017). As a human services professional, it is your role to become acquainted with the provincial or territorial regulations where you are employed. Unfortunately, in our line of work, protection orders are common.

Let's go back to Renée's story: what if there is a protection order against the father, but he is the one who is paying the child care fees? You can schedule a time for the father to drop off the payment when the child is not at the centre. The other options are to meet him offsite in a public location, or send him a self-addressed, stamped envelope so he can mail in the payment.

You need to inform the mother of the result of the **action plan** that was created in order to respect the conditions of the protection order. Ensure that you are kept up to date on any changes to the rulings by communicating with the custodial parent/guardian. There are many benefits to using action plans. It helps staff to develop a working relationship with the family and provides clarity in situations that could become complex—and for some individuals, even scary. When you are creating an action plan, you need to consider all possible scenarios. For example, the supervisor said she would meet the father offsite to collect the payment, but where and when? And how do you explain this to him? It is important to establish an objective, describe what will happen, and include strategies for achieving the objective. Be inclusive; everyone in your workplace needs to have a full understanding of the plan. You need to work as a team to set goals and understand the complexity of the situation. The goal is to respect the law and ensure the safety of the people in your care.

In this situation, you need to support the mother. You will have to reassure her that her son is safe and that she can trust the child care centre. You can do this by employing active listening techniques, such as showing empathy and validating her feelings (Media Education Foundation, 2005), keeping the lines of communication open, and providing regular updates on her son's progress. Utilizing these techniques will help strengthen your relationship and diminish the trust issues she is experiencing.

Depending on the age of the child, biting may be a stage of development. It is important for human services professionals to know the typical stages of development and be able to recognize when a child is not meeting their **developmental milestones**. There are a number of tools on the market to ensure this, including the Early Development Instrument (EDI), which is completed by kindergarten teachers across Canada (Offord & Janus, 2000), or Ages and Stages (ASQ-SE). Ages and Stages is a series of questionnaires designed to track children's development starting at two months of age and continuing every two months up to the age of five years (sixty months) (Squires, Twombly, Bricker, & Potter, 2009).

Scientists, doctors, parents, and early childhood specialists know that early detection of developmental delays is essential in order to intervene appropriately. Research has consistently shown that medical and biological indicators are not reliable predictors of infant outcomes, and that in order to provide effective early identification, a child's development needs to be monitored frequently (Pati, Hashim, Brown, Fiks, & Forrest, 2011). Usually a child is seen by a public health nurse during scheduled trips to the clinic for immunizations. After the age of eighteen months, children do not typically receive another vaccination until they are ready to start school. During that gap, it is difficult and costly for families to bring a child for an assessment by a multidisciplinary team on a regular basis. By administering the Ages and Stages questionnaires, rural clients, families, and health agencies can keep track of children's development more effectively (Squires et al., 2009, p. xii). The early childhood educator, public health nurse, early interventionist, human services professional, or health care professional fills out the first part of the questionnaire; the parents fill out the second part. The questionnaires are available in English, French, and Spanish. One of the authors (Mazerolle) administered the age-appropriate questionnaire when a child started at her centre and then every six months after that if she did not have any concerns. This also helped to inform her weekly planning. She noticed that the children in her care were having difficulty tracing around objects, so she added some opportunities to her programming to give them a chance to practice this skill. A tool such as the ASQ is important because the results help identify infants, toddlers, and young children who may benefit from early intervention programs (Squires et al., 2009, p. xvii). Canadian paediatricians also created a website called Caring for Kids. Designed for parents, it outlines the developmental milestones and recommends that parents speak with their doctor if they are concerned that their child "seems to be behind in more than one of the areas" that include gross motor skills, fine motor skills, social/language skills, and cognitive skills (Canadian Paediatric Society, 2014).

For example, sometimes children have speech delays and their parents are concerned. You need to observe the development of the whole child. Maybe they are going through a growth spurt and all of their energies are being directed to physical growth rather than intellectual growth. The author (Mazerolle) points out a case at her child care centre where a child was ignoring the educators and would not respond when they called her name. They believed that she was ignoring them and they implemented consequences. When the author observed what was happening, she noted that the girl only ignored the verbal commands from the educators when her back was to them. The author suggested that the parents take their daughter for a hearing test. The audiologist found that she was totally deaf in her right ear and only had 20% hearing in her left ear. This information certainly helped the educators and the parents to provide better quality care for the child and changed the way they interacted with her, making sure that she was facing them when they spoke. They also learned some sign language, which was beneficial to all the children at the centre.

Regardless of whether the negative behaviour is developmentally appropriate or not, you will have to work with the parents to help eliminate it. When a negative behaviour occurs—such as one child biting another—this is considered to be an incident. The staff member who witnessed the behaviour fills out an **incident report**, indicating the date and time of the incident and a description. No names are used (to protect the identity of the children who were involved), and both sets of parents receive and sign a copy of the report. A copy is kept on file and the licensing officer for your region needs to be informed of the incident. If there are too many incident reports, there will be an investigation of the program and facility.

Often parents fear that their child is being perceived as a "bad child" and therefore they are "bad parents" (Henninger, 2013, p. 184). This can lead to low self-esteem or trust issues. The parents may discipline the child at home for an incident that happened hours earlier, while the child was in care. If all the information you provide to a parent about their son or daughter is in the form of an incident report, all your hard work in developing the relationship with the parent will be in vain. You will have to develop a system where you counter the negativity of the report by sending positive messages home as well. It could be "I zipped up my coat all by myself." If you are faced with yet another incident report, work with the parent to explain what you have put into place to redirect the negative behaviour. In order to do this, you may need to assign a staff member to observe and document what led up to that behaviour. By analyzing the observations, you will be proactive and be able to intervene before the behaviour occurs again. For example, what led to the biting?

Often children are in close proximity to one another from a young age. Depending on a number of factors, including their stage of development, each child will be interacting socially with adults and children. These interactions can be positive, such as using their manners, sharing, and helping to clean up their toys; or negative, such as having a tantrum, throwing toys, pushing, or biting other children. Educators strive to give attention to the positive behaviours and minimize the attention they give to the negative behaviours. Thus, the child who was bitten receives a lot of hugs, and the child who bit will be asked to go get the ice pack to apply to the wound. There are social stories, such as Tucker the Turtle, that have been developed to help teach children about pro-social behaviour (Center on the Social and Emotional Foundations for Early Learning, 2017).

Share your documentation with the parents and involve them in the process. Together, you can create a plan so that you can be consistent at the centre as well as at home. An **inclusive care plan** is a document that will assist your program in developing interventions and creating relevant programming for each specific child. It is an industry document that follows different templates. The information found in the plan starts with the date and the name of the child. The next step is to list the interested parties. In this case, it would be the mother. Working together with the mother, you would list the child's strengths and identify their needs. In this case, the need is to learn more prosocial behaviours and self-regulation techniques. Every inclusive care plan will have an end goal, such as to curb biting and other **anti-social behaviours**. The goals need to be specific and measurable. For example, "The child will bite fewer than three times a day." You will need to meet with the parents in order to reassess the plan on a predetermined basis and readjust it as necessary. All parties sign the plan to indicate their willingness to adhere to it.

Although inclusive care plans are specific to one child, every child in the centre could benefit from learning self-regulation techniques, such as deep breathing, and from the opportunity to be by themselves as needed in order to avoid conflict (Shanker, 2016). One centre that one of the authors (Mazerolle) worked with had a tent set up in the corner. Another one had a teepee. The child could be by themselves but still be in ratio. Do not hesitate to make a **referral** when you feel you need additional support for the parent or the child. A referral may be necessary for the wellbeing of the child; it is not a sign of failure. Sometimes we want to solve everything ourselves when it really is not possible.

OPTION 2: RENÉE'S CHOICE

Well, let me tell you what I did. I re-engaged the child with his father. Lots of supports for mom, lots of referrals for mom, recommendations for counselling for mother and father. Their relationship was in a really bad place, and also getting mom to attempt to build a relationship with dad's new girlfriend. So that played another dynamic in it, and getting mom to learn how to trust him again, which was not easy, so we had to support that process. So if dad came to pick him up we would send mom a quick text message and say, "Yes, dad was on time to pick him up." It was all those little pieces of support that we didn't originally think of that took a whole process of "How do we support mom?" What does that look like, knowing mom didn't trust him? There was children's services involvement because we had to make sure dad was following what dad had to follow, make sure dad wasn't using drugs anymore, make sure dad wasn't abusive, and following his court orders and all of that. So we had to ensure that involvement was there, and it was pretty positive, there was nothing negative that came up on dad or his girlfriend. It probably took eight to ten months before mom was even willing to consider trusting us to support him in being a positive parent again. I think the one day that really changed things was the day I came in and the little guy says to me, "That's my dad, Ms. Renée!" and I said, "I know." He replied, "I love him!" and dad just lost it, broke down into tears, and thanked me for supporting that relationship. That was probably the best day I had at work.

As Renée said, in order to reintegrate the father into his son's life, you will need to support the mother by providing reassurance that her son is safe and that she can trust your centre. You can do this by employing active listening techniques, such as showing empathy and validating her feelings (Media Education Foundation, 2005); keeping the lines of communication open, even sending a text message like Renée did; and providing regular updates on her son's progress. Utilizing these techniques will help strengthen your relationship and diminish her trust issues within herself as well as with the father.

There are different types of families in this world. The nuclear family, consisting of two parents and one or more children, is becoming less and less common. Families now consist of married couples, common-law couples with or without children, same-sex families, single parents, foster families, grandparents-as-parents families, and blended families. There are many other examples. A key tip in human services is to remember that families do not need to be biologically related. Many Canadians choose who will be a member of their family in order to have a support network and a familial relationship. Typically this is referred to as a chosen family or street family, depending on the situation and the group of individuals involved.

Regardless of the type of families you are working with, Hattie's 2009 "Visible Learning" study found that

> parents have major effects in terms of the encouragement and expectations that they transmit to their children .... Across all home variables, parental aspirations and expectations for children's educational achievement has the strongest relationship with achievement ... thus ... schools need to work in partnership with parents to make their expectations appropriately high and challenging, and then work in partnership with children and the home to realize, and even surpass, these expectations. (p. 70)

In Renée's case, she can work with both parents, examining their parenting styles to help them better understand each other. Parenting styles are often defined along a continuum of responsiveness and behavioural control. The behavioural control is defined by the demands that parents make on children to become integrated into the family. The typology of parenting styles include authoritarian, authoritative, uninvolved, or indulgent (permissive). The **authoritarian** style is low parental responsiveness and high demands. Parents often tend to demand obedience and do not take their child's needs into consideration. The **authoritative** parenting style occurs when there is high parental responsiveness and high parental demands. These types of parents monitor their children and set standards that are assertive but not intrusive; the child will have support and not be subjected to punitive disciplinary methods. These types of parents encourage their children to be assertive, self-regulated, and socially responsible. **Uninvolved** parents are those with low responsiveness and low parental demands. Often the children are neglected. Parents who have an **indulgent** parenting style show high parental responsiveness and low demands. These parents are non-traditional and often seen as lenient. They do not require the children to mature in terms of their behaviour (Dental Abstracts, 2008, p. 30).

Now that we have discussed the parental dynamics, let's examine how we can support this family. You will have to work with both of the parents to help eliminate negative behaviours. Alberta, Manitoba, and Ontario support the Triple P Program (Positive Parenting Program), which was designed by Professor Matt

Sanders at the University of Queensland in Australia. These provinces offer workshops and training in the Triple P method to help parents develop their skills. The training focuses on five steps:

1. Create a safe, interesting environment so the children will be actively engaged and not look for conflict.
2. Have a positive learning environment. Boosting their self-esteem is key.
3. Use assertive discipline. Have clear expectations and limitations and follow through with consequences.
4. Have realistic expectations. Be aware of their developmental stage. Is it reasonable to expect a two-year-old to sit for 20 minutes?
5. Take care of yourself as a parent. You cannot take care of someone else if you do not take care of yourself. (Triple P International, n.d.)

The Triple P has also designed a program for Indigenous families, one for children with exceptionalities, one for children who are overweight (which focuses on lifestyle), and one for families going through separation or divorce.

Like parents, early childhood educators strive to maximize the attention they give to the positive behaviours the child exhibits and minimize the attention they give to the negative behaviours. Thus, the child who was bitten receives a lot of hugs, and the child who bit will be asked to go get the ice pack to apply to the wound as a natural consequence to their action. This example illustrates one of Alfred Adler's four goals of misbehaviour.

Table 13: The four goals of misbehaviour

Attention-getting	Seeks attention and service. Attention could be negative or positive.
Power	Wants to be the boss.
Revenge	Wants to hurt others or get even.
Display of inadequacy	Wants to be left alone. Don't make any demands on them.

Source: Dreikurs & Goldman, 1967

Once the early childhood educator identifies the goal behind the behaviour, they are better able to prevent it. According to Adler, a child's first goal is to get attention, and negative attention is just as good as positive attention. If their needs for attention are not met, they will escalate to a need for power (second goal), and finally for revenge (third goal). The fourth goal is a display of inadequacy, where the child acts helpless so others will do the work for them—during clean up time, for example (Dreikurs & Goldman, 1967). As early childhood educators, we need to tell children what we want to see to stop negative behaviours from the beginning. Thus we say, "Walk," rather than, "Don't run," or "No running." We also ask questions rather than using the word "no." For example, "Are you sitting on the chair?" Changing the language changes the tone of the message and clarifies our expectations for the children in our care.

If the issue is widespread, you could host a workshop for parents around certain key topics, such as potty training, in order to provide some information and a chance to discuss their challenges and successes with other parents. Send out an invitation and serve some snacks. You could also provide childcare in a separate room to enable more families to attend. If you do not feel comfortable discussing a topic, invite a guest speaker such as a public health nurse.

If a public forum creates some anxiety, you could meet with parents one-on-one for a parent conference. It is important to set up a parent conference to discuss the positive things you are seeing as well as the negative. You will need to invite the parents to come at a time that is convenient for them. Be sure to tell them why you called the meeting, and take notes during the meeting that you can type out and send to them afterwards outlining what was discussed and agreed upon to ensure you are all on the same page.

Start with the positive and establish a rapport to put the parent at ease. Ask questions so you give them a chance to speak and express their concerns, and really listen to what they have to say. You are looking for consistency between what is happening at the centre and what is happening at home. Always refer back to the policies, such as your parent handbook and the licensing act, to justify your decisions. Ask another employee to attend the meeting if you need a witness or a translator, or if you think there will be some issues with communication. You should also bring samples of the child's work or videos to illustrate the positive as well as your concerns.

Be careful with confidentiality. Discuss only their child; do not mention other children by name. You can include them in the pictures and video only if you have written permission from their parents or guardians. Make plans for helping the child at home and in the program, and establish a timeline when you will meet again to evaluate the plan by discussing the progress and challenges encountered. The parents should leave the meeting feeling supported rather than judged.

TIME TO DEBRIEF

Renée did not hesitate to make a referral when she felt the family needed additional support. A tip for success in this industry is to understand that there are a lot of supports available to our clients that we need to know about. Drive around your community and meet people, network, and find out what programs are available. Even if you have lived in a community your whole life, you will be surprised to discover what resources are available. Some referrals that are common in early intervention work could include counselling, the early intervention specialist, legal aid, financial aid, child and family services, or addiction programs. Hopefully you have noticed that all of these positions fall under the human services model for care, because, as an African proverb goes, "it takes a village to raise a child."

KEY CONCEPTS

Action plan
Anti-social behaviours
Authoritarian
Authoritative
Court order
Developmental milestones
Family law protection order
Incident report
Inclusive care plan
Indulgent
Peace bond
Referral
Restraining order
Uninvolved

IN THE PURSUIT OF KNOWLEDGE

1. It is closing time at the daycare. There is an incident report in the boy's locker. Role play a meeting between the mother and Renée in order to establish some measurable goals.
2. Brainstorm other positive behaviour techniques you could use when one child is hurt by another.
3. What are some parenting topics you can discuss at a workshop with the parents at the centre?

REFERENCES

Carr, M., & Lee, W. (2013). *Learning stories: Constructing learner identities in early education.* London: SAGE.

Center on the Social and Emotional Foundations for Early Learning. (2017). *Resources: Practical strategies for teachers/caregivers.* Retrieved from http://csefel.vanderbilt.edu/resources/strategies.html

Dental Abstracts. (2008). Paediatric dentistry: Parenting styles. *Dental Abstracts, 53*(1), 30–31.

Dreikurs, R., & Goldman, M. (1967). *The ABCs of guiding the child.* Retrieved from www.adlerian.us/guid.htm

Government of British Columbia. (2017). *Information on protection orders.* Retrieved from www2.gov.bc.ca/gov/content/safety/crime-prevention/protection-order-registry/qa

Hattie, J. (2009). *Visible learning: A synthesis of over 800 meta-analyses relating to achievement.* Oxford: Routledge.

Henninger, M. (2013). *Teaching young children: An introduction* (5th ed.). Englewood Cliffs, NJ: Pearson.

Media Education Foundation. (2005). *Techniques for active listening.* Retrieved from www.mediaed.org

Offord, D., & Janus, M. (2000). *Early development instrument.* Retrieved from https://edi.offord-centre.com/

Pati, S., Hashim, K., Brown, B., Fiks, A., & Forrest, C. (2011, August 18). Early identification of young children at risk for poor academic achievement: Preliminary development of a parent-report prediction tool. *BMC Health Services Research, 11*(197). http://dx.doi.org/10.1186/1472-6963-11-197

Shanker, S. (2016). *Think, feel, act: Lessons from research about young children.* Retrieved from www.edu.gov.on.ca/childcare/selfRegulate.html

Squires, J., Twombly, E., Bricker, D., & Potter, L. (2009). *Ages and stages questionnaires user's guide* (3rd ed.). Baltimore: Paul H. Brookes.

Triple P International. (n.d.). *5 steps to positive parenting.* Retrieved from www.triplep-parenting.ca/alb-en/get-started/5-steps-to-positive-parenting/

ISABELLE'S STORY

Hi! My name is Isabelle. I am involved in many aspects of the human services field. My paid position is at a men's shelter as an intake worker. I coordinate and process all the information for the homeless men who come into the shelter. I fill out and keep track of all of the paperwork and try to find them supports by locating appropriate programs to help them, such as housing, food bank, and detox services. I also have a part-time job as a float health care aid in the local hospital. My worst day was when I was working in the emergency department with my roommate, who is a nurse.

Summer's twins

Source: C. Genest

We had two siblings, a five-year-old girl and her twin brother. We had noticed in the past six months that the condition of the kids was deteriorating and they were making a lot of visits to the emergency department. At the beginning, we were seeing them once a month or once every six weeks, and suddenly it was weekly. Just before we reported them to child protection, it was every two to three nights; they were back in emerg all the time. We couldn't prove what we thought was happening, but we thought that the mother, Summer, was being abused by the kids' father. They were not married, they were just living together.

We were well aware that the father had a very high addiction to drugs, because he was one of our frequent fliers for drugs too. Summer was twenty-one years old. She was filthy, had no self-defense mechanisms, and very little self-esteem. I think she was probably suffering from depression too, because the kids were dirty and not appropriately dressed for the weather. The children were apathetic; they were not as joyful as they used to be. Their weight was going down instead of going up the way it should have been. They should have been developing and growing. Sometimes we would see a bruise like fingerprints on their arms. On their knees we would see bruises. The boy would say, "Daddy was mad and I had to be in the corner." We would see some bruises on their bums too. We could see that if someone in the waiting room was eating something, they were looking at it. We always have some food available. We would give them toast and jam, a glass of juice. It was like we had given them a big meal, they appreciated it so much.

We saw that the problem was getting worse and worse, so we reported them to child protection. We have a 1-800 number to call and the family was already on social assistance. Summer was known to them. They would visit infrequently; at the time everything was functioning well. We were guaranteed that the social worker would go to their apartment the next morning.

❦

You have two choices:

Option 1: Do not tell the mother that you have called social services. If you choose this option, turn to page **135**.

Option 2: Inform the mother that you have called social services. If you choose this option, turn to page **140**.

OPTION 1

In order for a child to survive and thrive into adulthood, their basic needs must be met. They need food, love, shelter, and protection. When these basic needs are met, they will be able to develop as healthy individuals both physically and mentally (Roesler & Jenny, 2009, p. 44). Unfortunately, this is not always the case. It is important to recognize the signs of abuse—what to look for and why—when you are working with people. It is also important to understand child maltreatment—the term used to include all the ways a child can be mistreated and hurt through acts of omission or commission.

There are many different types of abuse. **Financial or economic abuse** occurs when a person controls or takes advantages of another person's finances, steals from them, or preys on their insecurities about not having enough money. This form of abuse is often underreported and often occurs to seniors (Reeves & Wysong, 2010, p. 329). **Medical abuse** takes place when a guardian or caretaker is responsible for an individual receiving too much medical care, or care that they do not need that could cause them harm. It is important to note that this form of abuse refers only to harmful or unnecessary medical treatment (Roesler & Jenny, 2009, p. 45).

Neglect is evident in the case of the twins, who were dirty, hungry, and not wearing appropriate clothing for the weather. There are different types of neglect. Physical neglect is not protecting a child from physical harm. If you are aware that a child, a vulnerable person, or anyone at all is being physically harmed and do not report it, you could be charged. There is psychological neglect, which goes hand in hand with psychological abuse. Psychological neglect is failing to provide the basic emotional needs of a child or a vulnerable person (Roesler & Jenny, 2009, p. 44). Medical neglect occurs when a caretaker fails to bring a child to get care, but it is defined specifically as a child being deprived of necessary medical care (Roesler & Jenny, 2009, p. 45). It is a good sign that Summer knew she had to take the twins to the emergency department for treatment.

Physical abuse is not limited to children; it can happen to anyone regardless of age or sex. It is deliberate, physically violent actions towards an individual committed by a care provider, a partner, someone in a position of trust, or sometimes a stranger (Bilo, Oranje, Shwayder, & Hobbs, 2013, p. 1). The severity of the abuse may range from punching, beating, kicking, burning, or slapping. Children can be burned accidentally by hot liquids or stove tops. Suspicious types of burn mark "patterns seen can involve iron or cigarette burns and should raise concern for inflicted injury" (Toon et al., 2011). Physical abuse can have lethal consequences and may not always be visible (Bilo et al., 2013, p. 1). Typically, physical abuse is apparent by the placement of bruises on the child's body. It is important, as human services professionals, to note the placement of bruises, as some children who are learning to walk or playing sports often have bruises; these do not mean that they are being abused. Bruises that are commonly found on active children appear on the forehead, shins, and knees. Uncommon places for bruises are "on the back, or around the eyes or wrists" (Encyclopedia of Children's Health, 2017). The colour of the bruise is also important. As they heal,

> [b]ruises change colours over time in a predictable pattern, so that it is possible to estimate when an injury occurred by the colour of the bruise. Initially, a bruise will be reddish, the colour of the blood under the skin. After one to two days, the red blood cells begin to break down, and the bruise will darken

to a blue or purplish color. This colour fades to green at about day six. Around the eighth or ninth day, the skin over the bruised area will have a brown or yellowish appearance, and it will gradually fade back to its normal colour. (Encyclopedia of Children's Health, 2017).

If the parent says that their child fell off the swing on the weekend, the colour of the bruise should match the timeline, thus enabling you to verify the story. Physical abuse can also involve frequent fractures and shaking, which is especially harmful to the developing brain. This is referred to as shaken baby syndrome. **Shaken baby syndrome** can cause brain injury and even affect a child's vision (Kivlin, Simons, Lazoritz, & Ruttum, 2000).

In general terms, **sexual abuse** of a child is sexual contact that occurs under three conditions: when the act is done through deceit, trickery, or violence; when the perpetrator is in a position of authority over the child; and when there is a large age difference between the child and the perpetrator. It includes acts such as fondling; "sexual exploitation over the Internet; as well as exposing a child to, or involving a child in, pornography or prostitution" (Rimer & Prager, 2016, p. 6). The offender may make the child participate in inappropriate sexual behaviour by using threats, misrepresenting themselves, or even bribing them (Rimer & Prager, 2016, p. 7). The Criminal Code of Canada states that the age of consent is sixteen; however, someone who is twelve years old can consent under certain conditions to all forms of sexual activity (Justice Canada, 2016).

The recognition of what constitutes child abuse can change according to the cultural practices, norms, and political atmosphere of each society (Bilo et al., 2013, p. 1). As human services professionals, you will work with families from all over the world. For a new immigrant, something that was common in their country of origin, such as child brides, may be against the law in Canada. This knowledge may give you, as a service provider, a better understanding of the family's actions. It is important to work with the family to help them realize some of the legal implications of the abuse, as well as the consequences it could have on the health of the child, such as brain injuries, fractures, abdominal injuries, reproductive health problems, unwanted pregnancy, alcohol and drug abuse, cognitive impairment, poor relationships, low self-esteem, chronic lung disease, and liver disease (Bilo et al., 2013, p. 8).

We recommend that you become familiar with the **United Nations Convention on the Rights of the Child** (CRC or UNCRC). This document is the human rights treaty for children. Twenty-five years ago, the convention changed the way children were treated and viewed worldwide (UNICEF, 2017).

By understanding the CRC, you will become much more familiar with human rights. This is important not only when working with children but also with adult clients. As you read in Sara's story, every individual in the world has rights, and it is your role as a human services professional to know these rights and work within them, and to advocate for clients whose rights have been violated.

Like child abuse, **domestic violence** is prevalent worldwide. It has a profound impact on the emotional wellbeing, health, opportunities in life, and security of all individuals who live in the home with the abuser (Radford & Hester, 2006, p. 7). One misconception is that domestic violence takes place only within the home and only when a couple is in a relationship. This is not true; the violence can continue once the couple has separated (Radford & Hester, 2006, pp. 7-8).

You are not obligated to tell Summer that you reported her situation to social services. Social services is required by law to protect your identity so that there will not be repercussions towards you or your agency from the mother and/or father. "Every province and territory legislates the duty to report to the designated authority if a person suspects or believes that a child is being abused or is at risk of abuse" (Rimer & Prager, 2016, p. 96). If you fail to report abuse, you are breaking the law and could face jail time.

You are obligated by law to report abuse and are advocating for Summer and her children's welfare; however, if you tell her so, she might not see it that way. A common reaction to a report of abuse is to defend the abuser and blame oneself. Summer could also go out of her way to avoid you, and then not seek out help in the future if she believes she cannot trust you because you reported her to social services. As Isabelle explained, Summer may experience low self-esteem, a lack of self-defense mechanisms, and depression. As a result, it could be difficult to convince her to take the children and leave the father. However, Summer could also be charged with child abuse and neglect because, although she was not guilty of abuse, she did nothing to prevent it from happening.

According to Nova Scotia's Domestic Violence Resource Centre (2017), there are numerous barriers to leaving a violent relationship. They include limited access to information, lack of transportation, loss of community and support networks, and a distrust of the system. When services are accessible, Nova Scotia's Domestic Violence Resource Centre (2017) noted that the barriers to using them include fear of being misunderstood, lack of resources for support or treatment, services that are not culturally relevant, fear of the justice system, and wariness that personal issues will become public knowledge, especially in small communities.

Summer is from a small town, so Isabelle knows some of her history. She became pregnant with the twins at the age of 16. According to William, Sawyer and Wahlstorm (2013), many teen mothers become single parents, and half of the children of teen moms never live with their biological fathers. They also discuss how children of adolescent mothers are more likely to fail in school, have a higher likelihood of substance abuse, and are more likely to have problems with the law (Public Health Agency of Canada, 2017; William et al., 2013). There are several programs that support teen parents by providing care for their children while they return to school to obtain their high school diploma. Such supports include parenting classes, providing clothing and diapers as well as healthy food and infant formula, and cooking classes where they teach the mother how to cook for herself as well as make homemade baby food.

Summer could use a **support system** because her mother died last year. As a human services professional, it is important to understand that when working with someone who is in a stressful situation, has experienced a loss, or is facing a crisis, you need to be flexible and have a backup plan ready if your original plan does not work. Who else can Summer confide in and rely on who would be like a mother to her? Maybe a friend, a sibling, or an aunt? Maybe a professional such as a doctor or a counsellor?

She might need to see a professional for treatment if she is diagnosed with **depression**. Women are diagnosed twice as often as men (Martin, Neighbors, & Griffith, 2013, p. 1100). Some symptoms of depression include insomnia, sadness, irritability, anxiety, mood reactivity, appetite change (either loss of appetite or overeating), suicidal ideation, loss of sexual drive, panic, stomach problems, and energy loss (Fried, Epskamp, Nesse, Tuerlinckx, & Borsboom, 2016, p. 315). Sadness is a natural response to the loss of someone or something (a job, a relationship, a home, etc.), but there are many factors that influence a person's response to loss, such as the nature of the loss, the individual's coping skills, and access to support networks (Wood & Schweitzer, 2016).

The **five stages of grief**, introduced in 1969 by Elisabeth Kübler-Ross, are

1. Denial (shock)
2. Anger (with the situation, the doctor, or the person who passed away)
3. Bargaining (trying to negotiate with another person)
4. Depression
5. Acceptance (coming to terms with the situation)

Grief is a normal response to loss, but what are some coping strategies? Getting enough sleep, eating healthy, and trying to stay physically fit are a few. It is always a good idea to express emotions, acknowledge feelings and face them, reach out to others for support, see a counsellor, or join a support group. "Because grief is a highly individualised experience, the most effective grief support offers a range of options, including online support, bibliotherapy, individual counselling, group support, community support, rituals, and psycho-educational programs" (Hall, 2011). Summer would not only be helping herself to regain balance and live a healthy lifestyle but would also be setting an example for her children to do the same.

OPTION 2: ISABELLE'S CHOICE

We told the mother and she got really nervous and defensive. We told her that she didn't have a choice. Every visit to the emergency department was by ambulance because she didn't have to pay, and she knew the hospital staff wouldn't let her walk home with two children so we would give her a token for a free taxi ride. She was learning to use the system very well, as a matter of fact. It was very sad when you saw the children so dirty. They were two beautiful kids, it was just heartbreaking. We didn't have the right to follow up. After we referred them, we had a visit one night from Summer and her daughter, who had a bad ear infection, so it was justified. The visits became less frequent. The kids stayed in her custody, but they were supervised by social services every week, then every two weeks, then it was monthly.

Relationships are different worldwide and the value of women in society is very cultural. In some cases women are revered as the head of the household, and in others they are considered possessions. In some societies, women are violated because of their gender and discrimination is common practice. In others, a woman's virtue is considered extremely important and a depiction of the family's honour. As human services professionals, it is important to research different world views, cultures, and religions in order to understand what could possibly be happening in the woman or child's life. What may be acceptable in one country or society may not be acceptable in Canada. There have been honour killings in Canada, and women have been sent to another country to marry men against their wishes. You may experience gender discrimination yourself if you move away from Canada, or if you work with someone from another cultural background. Remember that education is the key, as this person may not know they are doing something that is against societal beliefs and values, or even against the law. A child does not choose their parents and might simply be following their example, which is why we sometimes see abuse as a cycle. For example, Michael's parents spanked him as a child, so when Michael grows up, the cycle will repeat itself if he spanks his children. Men can also be victims of abuse, rape, and discrimination if they do not appear to be following the customs of their society. Some men have been killed for being homosexual. You need to become self-aware and examine your own beliefs, as well as your values. Discover what is important to you and how you have been influenced by your upbringing. Lastly, become aware and have a good understanding of the **Universal Declaration of Human Rights** (see Table 14).

The recognition of what constitutes child abuse can change according to the cultural practices, norms, and political atmosphere of each society (Bilo et al., 2013, p. 1). As human services professionals, you will work with families from all over the world. For a new immigrant, something that was common in their country of origin, such as child brides, may be against the law in Canada. This knowledge may provide you with a better understanding of a family's actions. It is important to work with the family to help them to realize some of the legal implications as well as the consequences the abuse could have on the health of their child, such as brain injuries, fractures, abdominal injuries, reproductive health problems, unwanted pregnancy, alcohol and drug abuse, cognitive impairment, poor relationships, low self-esteem, chronic lung disease, and liver disease (Bilo et al., 2013, p. 8). It is also important to understand child maltreatment—the term used to include all the ways a child can be mistreated and hurt through acts of omission or commission. It is a good sign that Summer knew to take the children to the emergency room for treatment, but she needs to do more to protect them and herself.

You are not obligated to tell Summer that you reported her situation to social services. Social services is required by law to protect your identity to avoid repercussions towards you or your agency from the mother and/or father. "Every province and territory legislates the duty to report to the designated authority if a person suspects or believes that a child is being abused or is at risk of abuse" (Rimer & Prager, 2016, p. 96). If you fail to report abuse, you are breaking the law and could face jail time. You are obligated by law to report abuse in this case and are advocating for Summer and her children's welfare. However, when you tell her about the report, she might not see it that way. A common reaction to a report of abuse is to defend the abuser and blame oneself. Summer could also go out of her way to avoid you, and then not seek out help in the future if she believes that she cannot trust you because you reported her to social services.

Table 14: Universal Declaration of Human Rights

Article 1	Right to Equality
Article 2	Freedom from Discrimination
Article 3	Right to Life, Liberty, Personal Security
Article 4	Freedom from Slavery
Article 5	Freedom from Torture and Degrading Treatment
Article 6	Right to Recognition as a Person before the Law
Article 7	Right to Equality before the Law
Article 8	Right to Remedy by Competent Tribunal
Article 9	Freedom from Arbitrary Arrest and Exile
Article 10	Right to Fair Public Hearing
Article 11	Right to be Considered Innocent until Proven Guilty
Article 12	Freedom from Interference with Privacy, Family, Home and Correspondence
Article 13	Right to Free Movement in and out of the Country
Article 14	Right to Asylum in Other Countries from Persecution
Article 15	Right to a Nationality and the Freedom to Change It
Article 16	Right to Marriage and Family
Article 17	Right to Own Property
Article 18	Freedom of Belief and Religion
Article 19	Freedom of Opinion and Information
Article 20	Right to Peaceful Assembly and Association
Article 21	Right to Participate in Government and in Free Elections
Article 22	Right to Social Security
Article 23	Right to Desirable Work and to Join Trade Unions
Article 24	Right to Rest and Leisure
Article 25	Right to Adequate Living Standard
Article 26	Right to Education
Article 27	Right to Participate in the Cultural Life of Community
Article 28	Right to a Social Order that Articulates This Document
Article 29	Community Duties Essential to Free and Full Development
Article 30	Freedom from State or Personal Interference in the above Rights

Source: United Nations, 1948

It is important to realize that becoming a parent is an adjustment. The moment the child becomes a part of the family, the dynamic changes; after all, parenting is a 24-hour-a-day job that can be extremely rewarding but also difficult. Parents often take a prenatal course offered by public health to prepare for the birth of their child; however, courses on how to be an effective parent are rare and often in the form of workshops. Most new parents set expectations for themselves that can sometimes be unrealistic. First-time parents soon realize that no two children are the same and there is no instruction manual for parenting. New parents should be monitored and encouraged to join the parent and tot programs in their community. Sharing their experiences with others, and realizing that they are not alone, and that there are resources available, will help them build knowledge, skills, and confidence.

TIME TO DEBRIEF

Many positions in human services include working with individuals who access **social assistance**. Canada has one of the most advanced social assistance systems in the world. Our system can be traced back to the 1940s (Vivekanadan, 2002, p. 45). Like health and education, social assistance falls under provincial and territorial jurisdiction. Social assistance, which is more commonly referred to as welfare, provides benefits to individuals who qualify for support—for example, people who are unable to work. The social services are funded and delivered through the public sector, the private sector, or a private non-profit sector. Some services are free and fully funded by the government; others require full or partial payment based on the income of the recipient. If a person has to claim unemployment due to illness or retirement, social programs like employment insurance or old age security pay a portion of their income (Vivekanadan, 2002, pp. 48–49).

Think of social assistance as an umbrella with a number of services under it. To start, there is low-income support, which is what most people think of when they think of social assistance. There is also education, housing (public housing), and employment benefits (EI); health care; services for senior citizens (old age security); services for children and their families (child and family services); and services for people with disabilities. You will be working under this umbrella, so you need to become acquainted with your provincial/territorial government's programs and services in order to help your client access the pertinent services. As you have seen with Isabelle's story, often when you refer a client to a program, you may not be able to follow up to see if they are accessing it. It is important to make sure that you protect yourself by documenting everything about the referral, including the date and time and the name of the person you spoke to. Keep copies of referrals, complaints, and services you contacted in the client's file so that you know that you directed the client responsibly. Keep track of your communications in case something happens and you need to present or defend your actions in court. **Documentation** is the key to success in human services. It may take some time, but it is extremely important.

KEY CONCEPTS

Depression
Documentation
Domestic violence
Financial or economic abuse
Five stages of grief
Medical abuse
Neglect
Physical abuse
Sexual abuse
Shaken baby syndrome
Social assistance
Support system
United Nations Convention on the Rights of the Child
Universal Declaration of Human Rights

IN THE PURSUIT OF KNOWLEDGE

1. Reflect upon and list your values and beliefs.
2. Who would you consider to be part of your support system?
3. Isabelle states that the couple she worked with was not married. Research the definition for legal marriage, common-law marriage, and a couple cohabitating in Canada. Are there different legal implications to their marital status? What are their rights?

REFERENCES

Bilo, R., Oranje, A., Shwayder, T., & Hobbs, C. (2013). *Cutaneous manifestations of child abuse and their differential diagnosis: Blunt force trauma.* London: Springer.

Encyclopedia of Children's Health. (2017). *Bruises.* Retrieved from www.healthofchildren.com/B/Bruises.html

Fried, E., Epskamp, S., Nesse, R., Tuerlinckx, F., & Borsboom, D. (2016). What are good depression symptoms? Comparing the centrality of DSM and non-DSM symptoms of depression in a network analysis. *Journal of Affective Disorders, 189,* 314–320.

Hall, C. (2011). Beyond Kübler-Ross: Recent developments in our understanding of grief and bereavement. *InPsych, 33*(6). Retrieved from www.psychology.org.au/publications/inpsych/2011/december/hall/

Justice Canada. (2016). *Age of consent to sexual activity: Frequently asked questions.* Retrieved from www.justice.gc.ca/eng/rp-pr/other-autre/clp/faq.html

Kivlin, J., Simons, K., Lazoritz, S., & Ruttum, M. (2000). Shaken baby syndrome. *Opthalmology, 107*(7), 1246–1254.

Kübler-Ross, E. (1969). *On death and dying.* New York: Macmillan.

Martin, L., Neighbors, H., & Griffith, D. (2013). The experience of symptoms of depression in men vs women: Analysis of the National Comorbidity Survey Replication. *JAMA Psychiatry, 70*(10), 1100–1106.

Nova Scotia Advisory Council on the Status of Women and the Government of Nova Scotia. (2017). *Nova Scotia Domestic Violence Resource Centre.* Retrieved from www.nsdomesticviolence.ca

Public Health Agency of Canada. (2017). *Teen pregnancy.* Retrieved from www.phac-aspc.gc.ca/hp-ps/dca-dea/stages-etapes/ado/pregnancy-grossesse-eng.php

Radford, L., & Hester, M. (2006). *Mothering through domestic violence.* London: Jessica Kingsley Publishers.

Reeves, S., & Wysong, J. (2010). Strategies to address financial abuse. *Journal of Elder Abuse & Neglect, 22*(3–4), 328–334.

Rimer, P., & Prager, B. (2016). *Reaching out: Working together to identify and respond to child victims of abuse.* Toronto: Nelson.

Roesler, T., & Jenny, C. (2009). *Medical child abuse: Beyond Munchausen syndrome by proxy.* Elk Grove Village, IL: American Academy of Pediatrics.

Toon, M. H., Maybauer, D. M., Arceneaux, L. L., Fraser, J. F., Meyer, W., Runge, A., & Maybauer, M. O. (2011). Children with burn injuries: Assessment of trauma, neglect, violence and abuse. *Journal of Injury and Violence Research, 3*(2), 98–110.

UNICEF. (2017). Convention on the rights of the child. Retrieved from www.unicef.org/crc/

United Nations (1948). The universal declaration of human rights. Retrieved from http://www.un.org/en/universal-declaration-human-rights/

Vivekanandan, B. (2002). The welfare state system in Canada: Emerging challenges. *International Studies, 39*(1), 45–63.

Williams, B., Sawyer, S., & Wahlstorm, C. (2013). *Marriages, families and intimate relationships* (3rd ed.). Englewood Cliffs, NJ: Pearson.

Wood, J., & Schweitzer, A. (2016). *Everyday encounters* (5th ed.). Scarborough, ON: Nelson.

CONCLUSION: JAMAL'S STORY

Hi! My name is Jamal. I am the director of recreation at a seniors' assisted living facility, which houses people who are transitioning from independent living. The residents here live in their own units with furniture from their homes, have access to a nurse 24 hours a day, and have the option of catered meals. Assisted living facilities are often attached to long-term care facilities for clients who are not able to live independently.

I am responsible for planning and implementing activities for residents that target their health and overall wellbeing. I interact with the residents to keep them socially active and engaged. I accomplish this by organizing activities such as scrapbooking, yoga, concerts, and trips to community events.

There was one resident, a man named Friedrich, who never participated in the activities and spent a lot of time alone in his room. One day, I decided to pay him a visit. When he opened the door, I noticed that he had been crying. I asked him what was wrong. He said that today was his parents' wedding anniversary and that he was thinking about them. I asked him to tell me about his parents and he began to reminisce.

Friedrich
Source: C. Genest

I was born in Lodz, Poland, in 1934. My parents were German and there were 200,000 Germans living in this city of 600,000. The Germans had their own schools, churches, and hospitals. My parents owned a grocery store on the busy main street of this city. Since they both worked in the store along with two employees, they hired a maid to look after the apartment, which was above the store, as well as my sister and me.

In 1939, when Germany invaded Poland, my father was drafted into the German army. At Christmas in 1944, the fighting came close to Lodz. Seeing as we were Germans in a Polish city, my mother decided it would be safer for us in Germany. But there were no more trains running, so we loaded some of our belongings onto a sleigh and started to walk. Since it was very cold, my mother wore her fur coat. She had sewn her jewellery into the lining of this coat. The jewellery would later be exchanged for food. My uncle had come, with his horse and wagon, to pick us up.

The highway was congested with refugees on foot, and in cars, wagons, and other army vehicles. After struggling for two days, my uncle convinced an army officer to allow my family to ride on top of one of the open trucks. Two days later, the army trucks ran out of gas. Again, we were lucky; we were able to get on a train leaving for Berlin. The train was very crowded and there was little food available.

When we arrived in Berlin, we experienced our first air raid, which was very frightening. The next day we arrived in Hochenstein Ernstall, where my uncle had arranged for a small apartment for me, my mother, and my sister. We had a hard time there. Food was very scarce. Six days a week, I would walk to the surrounding farms to beg for potatoes, which were our main staple. We stayed there until September 1945, when we received a letter from my uncle, who had settled in West Germany close to the border of East Germany, saying that we should go there because food was more plentiful. My uncle owned a bakery and he had bribed a Russian border guard with some vodka to bring my mother, my sister, and me across the river dividing East and West Germany in a rowboat.

We travelled on the running board of a very crowded train, holding our packsacks between our feet. We had been warned to get off the train on the outskirts of Hirschberg because the Russians were not allowing anyone to cross the border. Under cover of darkness, we went to the home of a lady who would bring us to the river to meet the Russian soldier. This lady told us that the soldier had been transferred and she didn't have another contact, so we had to return the same way we had come, and were happy to find that our apartment was still vacant.

After a month or so, my uncle sent another letter saying that another contact had been made, so we returned again to the lady's home. In the middle of the night, she took us down to the river to the waiting Russian soldier, who took us across the river in a small rowboat. The water was very still and the border guards on the bridge could hear the oars in the water. Although they could see nothing, they fired their rifles but were not able to hit the boat. On the other side of the river waited my uncle, who took us to his home. My aunt had a big bowl of freshly baked rolls and jam waiting for us, and told us to eat as much as we wanted. I could hardly believe my ears after being hungry for ten months. We rented an apartment there, and after two years my father returned. We hadn't seen him for four years.

Each individual life is made up of choices. The choices we make will have an impact not only on our lives, but on the lives of future generations. Some choices are risky—leaving home as a single parent with two young children, or taking a rowboat in the darkness of night. It takes courage to make the decision to leave our comfort zone and head in a new direction. How did you, the reader, choose between Option 1 and Option 2? Did you go by instinct? What influenced your decision? The lessons we learn from the choices we make will influence our practice and make us question our values and beliefs. They help us to grow as both a person and a professional.

Sometimes we are overwhelmed by the enormity of a situation and feel helpless. One person can make a difference. If Friedrich's uncle had not reached out, a whole branch of his family tree could have been lost. He had re-established his life as the owner of a bakery and was safe. What made him take the risk to contact the Russians to arrange the safe passage of his brother's family?

As human services professionals, we find ourselves in similar circumstances. We put our reputations on the line when we stand up for our beliefs and advocate for the wellbeing of our clients. By knocking on Friedrich's door, Jamal gained insight into him as a person and could then use this opportunity to create a connection with him. They talked about what Friedrich liked to do, and Jamal was able to incorporate Friedrich's ideas into his planning. He, in turn, came out of his room and joined in when Jamal organized a shuffleboard tournament. He even won!

It takes time to really listen to someone and see below the surface. Getting someone to trust you enough to open up about their past and listening without judgement is not easy. Even if someone made mistakes, it is important that they know it is not too late to change their destiny and leave a legacy for future generations. These lessons will help to shape the field of human services and may even change laws or practices in the future.

Typically the human services field focuses on children, vulnerable youth, and families. However, the Canadian population is growing older by the day and the birth rate is declining. With this trend, many individuals who have spent their career working specifically with children are now transitioning into employment opportunities with our elderly population. For the human services worker, this can be a learning curve. You now need to focus your attention on things that you would not even need to consider when working with a younger population—for example, end-of-life planning.

When working with seniors there are a few things to consider. The first is planning for their future. This can be a difficult task, especially for people who have spent the majority of their lives in their own house. How would you feel if you were told you could not live in your home anymore? It is important to have a conversation (in some cases many conversations will be needed) about their future. There could be a concern about safety; or maybe their life partner has died, leaving them to manage the house on their own.

Once the client has decided on the best course of action for them, it is time for you to make a plan. Always involve the client in the plan. Make a list of what they are looking for. Encourage them to take a tour of some of the local housing facilities and select their favourite. The facility where you work could host a tea time for future clients. This would give them the opportunity to get acquainted with the surroundings and speak with the residents to see if they would recommend living there. Remember, the earlier a person takes the step towards making a plan, the better.

Now that you have decided on an action plan for housing, it's time to consider end-of-life last wishes. What exactly is this? It includes decisions such as what the client's funeral will look like and where it will be. Do they have a will? If so, where is it kept? These are hard conversations. They can be very upsetting for some individuals, but they do not have to be stressful. Ask these questions in a non-threatening way. Just like you created a plan for housing, make a plan for end-of-life arrangements, in conjunction with the funeral home and/or a lawyer.

When someone no longer works and still lives in their home, they run the risk of social isolation. An individual may become isolated because of deteriorating health issues or for financial reasons. When a senior socially isolates themselves, they put themselves at risk. Companionship is important for numerous reasons. People have the right to a relationship with a friend or a partner. It keeps an individual physically, emotionally, and cognitively active and provides a reason for living. Social isolation can lead to accidents like a fall, poor mental and physical health, premature death (from a heart attack without assistance or dementia that is undetected), and suicide.

When you are worried about a client who is experiencing or at risk of social isolation, make a plan with them to diminish the likelihood that they will isolate themselves. Maybe organize some free events so that financial burdens are not a barrier. Provide transportation to make the events more accessible so clients will be more likely to attend and benefit from it. Some high schools organize lunches or band concerts and invite the seniors in their neighbourhood to attend. Many daycares and pre-schools are located in the same building as a long-term-care facility. According to Dr. Samir Sinha, director of geriatrics at Mount Sinai Hospital in Toronto, "volumes of research show that seniors who are socially engaged have better health. They are less likely to feel lonely or depressed and tend to have lower blood pressure and delayed cognitive decline. There is growing interest and support for what we call intergenerational activities—the concept of bringing the generations together to promote intergenerational connectivity. It can also help to fight ageism" (Monsebraaten, 2016). Therefore, it is a huge benefit to clients at both ends of the age spectrum.

Ageism is discrimination based on someone's age. Discrimination and abuse are often a sad reality of our work, and this is the case when working with seniors. Elder abuse can be financial, physical, mental, and sexual. The key to working with abuse cases is locating adult protective services in your community in order to ensure that your clients have access to help. If your community does not have an adult protective services division, you can call the police department and ask them to conduct a welfare check.

There is a re-occurring theme to this section: respecting the senior client by allowing them to make choices about their own lives. This can diminish a lot of anxiety about their final years on this earth. When the client feels they have some control over what happens to them, they experience some peace of mind. It is important that they feel supported but not overwhelmed. Transitions are stressful, and for some people the fear of the unknown upon death is terrifying. Taking the time to really listen and providing them with some resources and connections to others who are going through the same life changes can help ease your client's anxiety.

As you have seen throughout the book, we and our clients can travel down many different pathways. The work of human services professionals is based on the life cycle, which begins before birth and never truly ends. Our life experiences shape who we are and the choices we will make. Our role is to help individuals who are at risk in order to minimize or prevent the long-term consequences of their circumstances. We all make choices based on our circumstances, which can change in the blink of an eye. But the resources we have and the knowledge we gain will help us be successful mentors, leaders, and human services professionals. Friedrich, in his golden years, was still being impacted by the trauma he experienced as a child. *The Mentors Among Us* was created to provide a foundational resource to reassure you, the human services practitioner, that you are not alone in your journey. Always remember that your work matters. There will always be tragedy and happiness in the world. It is up to us, as human services professionals, to learn from the mentors among us and then determine how we can make a difference.

One day a man was walking along the beach when he noticed a boy picking something up and gently throwing it into the ocean. Approaching the boy, he asked, "What are you doing?" The youth replied, "Throwing starfish back into the ocean. The sun is up and the tide is going out. If I don't throw them back, they'll die." "Son," the man said, "don't you realize there are miles and miles of beach and hundreds of starfish? You can't possibly make a difference!" The boy bent down, picked up another starfish, and tossed it back into the surf. Then, smiling at the man, he said, "I made a difference for that one." (Adapted from "The Star Thrower" by Loren Eiseley, *The Unexpected Universe*, 1969)

REFERENCE

Monsebraaten, L. (2016, February 9). Magic abounds when daycare, seniors' home share roof. *The Toronto Star*. Retrieved from www.thestar.com/news/gta/2016/02/09/magic-abounds-when-daycare-seniors-home-share-roof.html

APPENDICES

APPENDIX A: ACCIDENT/INCIDENT REPORT

Client's name: _____

Date of accident/incident: _____

Time of accident/incident: _____

Observed and report prepared by: _____

Parent/guardian notified (date and time): _____

Cause of injury:
- ☐ Fall from _____
- ☐ Collision with _____
- ☐ Struck by _____
- ☐ Swallowed _____
- ☐ Other _____

Nature of injury:
- ☐ Scrape/scratch
- ☐ Bruise/bump
- ☐ Cut
- ☐ Nose bleed
- ☐ Bite
- ☐ Burn
- ☐ Object in eye/ear/nose
- ☐ Sprain
- ☐ Other _____

Location of accident/incident:
- ☐ Playground
- ☐ Room
- ☐ Gymnasium
- ☐ Hallway
- ☐ Stairs
- ☐ Washroom
- ☐ Field trip
- ☐ Other _____

Treatment administered by _____:
- ☐ First aid
- ☐ CPR
- ☐ None
- ☐ Sent home
- ☐ Sent to hospital

Part of body injured:
- ☐ Abdomen
- ☐ Ankle
- ☐ Arm
- ☐ Back
- ☐ Chest
- ☐ Ear
- ☐ Elbow
- ☐ Eye
- ☐ Face
- ☐ Finger
- ☐ Foot
- ☐ Hand
- ☐ Head
- ☐ Knee
- ☐ Leg
- ☐ Mouth
- ☐ Nose
- ☐ Scalp
- ☐ Tooth
- ☐ Other _____

Describe how accident/incident occurred: _____
_____
_____
_____

Parent/guardian signature: _____
Date: _____

APPENDIX B: BEHAVIOUR REPORT

Client's name: _____

Date: _____

Time: _____

Staff member's name: _____

Description of behaviour:
☐   Self-injury
☐   Self-stimulation
☐   Disruptive
☐   Inappropriate
☐   Unsafe
☐   _____

Location: _____

Activity:
☐   Arrival
☐   Transition _____
☐   Departure
☐   Individual
☐   Small group
☐   Large group
☐   Special activity
☐   Meal
☐   Self-care
☐   Other _____

Others involved:
☐   Peers
☐   Staff
☐   Family/guardian
☐   None

Strategy/consequence:

☐   Verbal reminder
☐   Redirection
☐   Removal of item
☐   Removal from activity
☐   Ignored behaviour
☐   Curriculum modification
☐   Time with staff
☐   _____

Describe what led up to the behaviour: _____
_____
_____
_____
_____

Reflection: How did my actions incite the behaviour? What could I have done to prevent the behaviour? _____
_____
_____
_____
_____

Staff member's signature: _____
Date: _____

APPENDIX C: ACTIVITY OUTLINE

Child's age: _____

Observation:

_____
_____
_____
_____

Connection to SPLICE:

_____
_____
_____
_____

Material:

_____
_____
_____
_____

Procedure:
Invitation/provocation

_____
_____
_____
_____

Body

_____

_____

_____

_____

Conclusion (extension)

_____

_____

_____

_____

_____

Self-evaluation/meaning making:

_____

_____

_____

_____

APPENDIX D: CASE PLAN TEMPLATE

Name: _____

Age/Date of birth: _____

Case plan goal(s): _____

Cultural background: _____

Language(s) spoken: _____

Strengths in the individual that may help with the goal	Concerns with the individual that may interrupt the goal

Who created the case plan?		
Name:	Position:	

Did the client participate in the creation of the case plan?	Yes	No
If yes, how?		
If no, why not?		
What are the three priorities identified in this plan?		

Issues or concerns about the client		Issues or concerns about the client		
Objectives	Actions to assist in solving concerns	Responsibility of the client	Time frame	Responsibility of the worker

EDUCATION		☐ No action required		
Issues or concerns about the client		The client's strengths		
Objectives	Actions to assist in solving concerns	Responsibility of the client	Time frame	Responsibility of the worker

EMOTIONAL AND BEHAVIOURAL FUNCTIONING (include abuse/neglect)	☐ No action required			
Issues or concerns about the client	The client's strengths			
Objectives	Actions to assist in solving concerns	Responsibility of the client	Time frame	Responsibility of the worker

FAMILY RELATIONSHIPS AND CONTACTS	☐ No action required			
Issues or concerns about the client	The client's strengths			
Objectives	Actions to assist in solving concerns	Responsibility of the client	Time frame	Responsibility of the worker

LIVING SKILLS AND SELF-CARE	☐ No action required			
Issues or concerns about the client	The client's strengths			
Objectives	Actions to assist in solving concerns	Responsibility of the client	Time frame	Responsibility of the worker

KEY ISSUES FOR REVIEW	NEXT REVIEW DATE

Prepared by: _____ Date: _____

Approved by: _____ Date: _____